Just Words
Who Will Teach Our Women??

A Musical Book/Message By:
Leslie Williams, Jr.

Music/Poetry by:
Kleva Talent

Cadmus Publishing

www.cadmuspublishing.com

Copyright © 2021 Leslie Williams, Jr.

Published by Cadmus Publishing
www.cadmuspublishing.com
Port Angeles, WA

ISBN:978-1-63751-115-2

All rights reserved. Copyright under Berne Copyright Convention, Universal Copyright Convention, and Pan-American Copyright Convention. No part of this book may be reproduced, stored in a retrieval system, or transmitted in any form, or by any means, electronic, mechanical, photocopying, recording or otherwise, without prior permission of the author.

"Look Lord, I done fucked up my life
And I didn't need anyone's help.
I did it AAALLLLLL by myself."
LESLIE WILLIAMS, JR.

"A woman's beauty is her power,
And she only becomes more and more powerful every day."
KLEVA TALENT

"When you appear to be strong, physically, mentally, spiritually, financially, people search for your weaknesses; but when you already appear to be weak or defeated, people often underestimate your strengths."
LESLIE WILLIAMS, JR.
AKA Kleva Talent

"Such is the way of an adulterous woman, she eats, and wipes her mouth, and says I have done no wickedness."
PROVERBS 30:20

FORWARD

Dear Women,

Let me start by saying I am not a religious person. I'm just a man that believes in God and His word. I wrote this book to you women because men of this world desire women to be ignorant. Ignorant about themselves. Ignorant about things in this world that exist, which they encounter every day, yet they don't even know that they are ignorant to them. And ignorant about their role in God's plan.

When a woman is ignorant about her true worth, and her true value, she allows herself to be manipulated, abused, and taken for granted because she thinks that it's normal. And often she even thinks she deserves it.

This book will help women to change all that. But only if you want it to.

It won't be easy. In fact, it's probably going to be the hardest thing you will ever do, including fighting for your right to vote, and bearing/raising children. But the reward will be far greater than anything you have ever known.

PROLOGUE

Just Words (Just Listen) [94 Tempo]
By Leslie Williams, Jr. aka Kleva Talent
2020 Copyright
Noted notes: ♮ = full rest; comma = ¼ rest; - = hold for 2 beats;
_ = hold for 1 beat.

i – grew up (up) ♮♮♮♮
shout out to the masterful Jon Voight ♮♮♮♮♮
it's not who we become _
it's who we were which is _
the per,son that we're runnin' from ♮ no one considers that ♮
no one considers ♮♮ no one considers Him ♮
no one considered me ♮ no one considered my enemy,
daily chasin' me apparently arrogant
deceptively made me believe i could control how high i get, ♮
a menace so society's violently eyein' me
angrily I respond wit' conduct conducive to drivin' me,
far away ♮
from love women and mi privado
yet if i recapture my freedom i'm a still be denied those _
every breath, and step i take,
makes me real ize
all of the foolish decisions i've made and still make
'cause when we sleep on the simple but, ♮

powerful trials of life,
we fall victim to the wrath and strife,
and it's aw,ful lonely
when you can't rely on the people you trust, ♮
and you can't get no time with the people you crushed,
wit' lies hate ♮ envy and an ger
and in the center of it all we're just, stran gers
estrange d from the womb it, self,
the cops, al ways assume
we'll forever be consumed wit' wealth,
but dealin' wit' drugs helped me learn my worth,
'cause since the day of my birth,
my laugh,ter was always strain ed and terse,
it's like my name was cursed,
that's why my lyrical is so, far from typical
10 percent strong 90 percent, vulner'ble
until i die ♮ so let's, celebrate my, death,
i know it won't, take you long to for, get, me ♮
but i know the world won't, rest
until it takes, my, breath,
that's why i'm waitin' on my Lord to come, get, me ♮
besides i'm ex ♮ as perated my rep a, 'sas sinated
i'm obsolete all i have are visions of girls i dated
and thoughts of women i wanna love ♮
but how selfish would it be
for me to ask them to trust, me ♮ who am i ♮
who am i ♮ ♮ who am i ♮ ♮
who am i ♮ ♮ who am i ♮ ♮ ♮ ♮
these words i write aren't Just, words they're Just, words
and i'm an artist so i'm a give you more than Just, words ♮
'cause i'm not Just, another body in prison
that Just happened to put his faith
in Just another religion Just listen ♮ ♮ ♮ ♮ ♮
Just listen babe ♮ Just listen ♮ ♮ Just listen
a million lies will criticize the enterprise
until it can no longer be recognized as advertised ♮

dehumanitized and denied acceptance
by everyone who claims to be empathetic ♮ unhypothetic ♮
got shattered hopes, and dreams ‿
sometimes i grieve sometimes i'm indignant
maybe that's how it's all intended ♮
'cause why would i ever do it, how could i be ♮ so stupid ♮
now i'm all alone in the dark ♮ wit' broken heart ♮
which i protected relentlessly through the solace of drugs
but i'm older so now reality took off the kiddie gloves ♭ ♮
where is my chance, at love where is my candy crush ♮
will she love me like i love her or am i askin' for too much ♮
i get attached, too easy give up too ea sy
'cause i refuse to compete for a woman that doesn't need me
This, too ♮ is meaningless, like chasin' the wind ♮
How many rounds with life is it gon' take me to win ♮
i want, somethin' better, but don't know where to begin,
when i walk along the streets they lead me back to the Penn ♮
but i can't ♮ vanish ♮ the world, needs me believe me
but why would they ever listen to me ♮ ♮
the beauty of a woman's laugh i will cherish eternally
but why will one ever want to love me ♮ who am i ♭ ♮
who am i ♭ ♮ who am i ♭ ♮ who am i who am i ♭ ♮
i grew up
these words i write aren't Just, words they're Just, words
and i'm an artist so i'm a give you more than Just, words ♭
'cause i'm not Just, another body in prison ♮ ♮ ♮
Just listen babe ♭ Just listen as times change
prison couldn't kill me it made me strange ♭
but life continues to taunt me i'll never be the same ♭
still these amateurs doubt me if ands about me
they couldn't even put their finger on the problem wit' out me
i've tasted the icy flames been tethered wit' chains ♭
now obsolescence is the cause erasin' my name ♭
but that's cool love conquers all of that ♮
but who wins this, war ‿
i thought i wouldn't have to sin, no, more ‿

when i met, you ♭ ♭
but you were hopin' i was somebody else ♭
this, too ♭ is meaningless, i'm chasin' the wind ♭
how many rounds wit' life, is it gon' take me to win ♭
Just listen babe ♭ Just listen ♭ ♭ Just listen

Contents

PART ONE ....

Chapter One 1

Chapter Two 6

Chapter Three 13

PART TWO 23

ACCOMPANIMENT ONE 23

ACCOMPANIMENT ONE (Part two) 25

Chapter One 27

Chapter Two 33

Chapter Three 43

Chapter Four 55

PART THREE 63

ACCOMPANIMENT TWO 65

Chapter One 71

PART ONE

YOU DON'T KNOW MY GOD

Chapter One

Dear Women,
    There are three things that I believe every woman should know:

1) What love truly is. And how to recognize, receive, and reciprocate it.

2) How to fight. I do not mean the feeble knee to the groin and run technique. Nor the panicky keys to the eyes/face attempt that can be smelled coming from thirty yards away. I'm talking about EVERY girl and woman being instructed on how to take on an attacker and successfully put that attacker on his (or her) ass, gasping for breath and/or pleading for medical attention. Women are built for grace and flexibility, but these together would also produce speed and power, you just need instruction on how to cultivate and harness them, and,

3) Who God truly is.

During my observations of the relationships between women and men I discovered that majority of the women I have encountered, and still encounter to this day, do not truly know who God is. And I also discovered that most men do not want their women to know God. In fact, they do not want their women to know any of the three things I mentioned above. And I am going to tell you why. But first, I want to clarify that when I say 'Know God' I am not saying that you should start going to church or start taking an interest in some religious faction simply because your man, your friends, or even I, say you should. All I am asking is for you to do your own research. Find out who God is and what His word says for yourself. Do not just rely on the word of someone who appears to be religious or has some religious information or insight. Nor should you just accept something as true simply because someone you know, or respect says it is true. People often make the mistake of allowing the opinions of others to be the foundation of their own beliefs instead on researching the information themselves. They do not consider that their friend's opinion or interpretation could have been cultivated while relying on false information. All I am saying is, make your own effort to get to know God. Put in the work. Do not just turn your back on Him because of the theories and opinions of others. Do not give up on Him without giving Him a chance to know you.

So, why won't men teach their women about love, fighting, and/or God? The answer is: Power and Control. Men of the world need women to be ignorant about themselves and their role in God's plan. When a woman is ignorant about her worth and her value within a relationship, she allows herself to be manipulated, abused, and taken for granted.

If your man does not know God, then he is not going to know how to truly love you or anyone else. Also, if your man does not know how to fight, you certainly cannot expect him to teach you. But I am talking about the man who knows what he is supposed to do in a relationship, but he is with a woman who does not know her own worth. And instead of showing the woman her value by respecting and loving her, he treats her like crap because he knows she will allow it.

Let us look at chivalry as an example. Most woman try to raise their sons to be gentlemanly and chivalrous. But if these traits are not part of his core belief system and he meets a woman that does not require him to be chivalrous, then he will probably opt to forego the chivalry. But for the man who knows how to love his woman, he understands that chivalry is just a natural manifestation of that love.

But if you do have a strong relationship with your man and he does know how to fight, then tell him to teach you. But please ladies, do not ask your man to teach you how to fight if he is abusing you. For he will only use it as an opportunity to abuse you further. And the only thing you will learn is how to be his punching bag. Instead, go to someone else, like a school. Or someone who can fight that you trust. Then have him or her teach you.

And I do not mean some yellow belt x-black crap, or some basic how-to-take-a-knife-from-your-opponent bullshit. I am talking about some real live down and dirty, knock down-drag out, how-to survival skills. Then the next time your so-called man wants to bully you and knock you around the house you will be able to WHUP-HIS-ASS and throw his ass out.

But do not learn how to fight just so you can bully your man around like he used to do to you. Fighting should only come as a last resort. And then only for defensive purposes. If your instructor is any good this should be one of the first things, he or she teaches you. but when the time comes for you to use what you have learned, DO NOT HOLD BACK. Remember J-Lo in 'Enough'? Master your body and your emotions, including your fear. Do not let fear cause you to get stiff or freeze up.

But again, fighting should only come as a last resort. And only when you are *forced* into defending yourself. No one is expendable. We should never embrace the philosophy that men or women are a dime a dozen. In fact, I encourage all women and men (especially couples who have kids together), to work out their differences if at all possible. And to fortify their relationships and their families.

For it is the lack of a Godly presence in our lives, and a blatant and callous disregard for one another which has caused our world to be in its current state.

Now I am going to be honest with you. There are a lot of things that I am going to say in this book that you are not going to like or agree with; but I am not saying them to make you happy. I am saying them because it is what you need to hear.

Other men will not tell you these things because they fear that telling you the truth and talking to you about God will only get in the way of them having sex with you.

People are always talking about changing the world and how their generation, this generation, or the next generation will be the one to finally do it. People love to emphasize that the children and their futures are what is the most important factor in bringing about world change. But if you do not know God, and you do not have the knowledge to teach your children about God, then you have already failed your generation, this generation, the next generation, and your children.

People believe that if we come together as a group, or as a 'movement' to tackle some of the issues we face in the world today we will make the fight that less strenuous for the people of tomorrow, which sounds noble and promising the theory, but the problem is that the issues which plague our civilization are only symptoms of the sickness which has permeated generation after generation since the beginning of time. And that sickness is that we do not want to know God. We have no interest in what He says or in how He wants us to live.

People argue that they are not religious, or that they do not have time for God; that the concerns of everyday life are more important than building a relationship with God. Which is ironic when you consider that it was Him who made it possible for us to have an everyday life. Without God there would not be any life. Yet we are arrogant enough to believe that we can get through this life, this gift, and find answers to all our problems without Him.

When we do this, we are telling God that we do not need Him. That our careers, or families and friends, and people who understand or can relate to our issues is all we need. We have even gone as far as to say that we do not need love. And these are the reasons why the world is the way it is today. And the reason it will only grow worse in future generations if we do not change.

A Godless and loveless world cannot and will not survive mankind's greed, lust for power, envious thoughts, jealous motives, and indifference to the needs of others. There are people who truly want to make the world better for all races, backgrounds, and genders. But for every one of us who are either caring, philanthropic, or edifying, there are fifty of us who just could not care less. This is a losing fight. And unless we change that the numbers are only going to get worse in the future generations, not better.

But how do we change it? How do we make things better not just for some, but for everyone? Well, that is the reason God has been urging me to write this book.

See, women have given up on not only God and love, but they have also given up on their role in God's plan.

If you were to ask one hundred women whether they would prefer love or happiness, seventy to eighty-five of them would choose happiness. Women do not have any faith in love anymore because they do not recognize it. Women and men usually associate the word love with things like gratitude, compromise, un-fulfillment, and even UN-happiness. Women and men look at love and marriage as an ordeal, or as if it's a sentence to spend life with only one sexual partner. They do not see love and marriage as being attributes of a committed and fulfilling, happy relationship.

So why write to the women? Why not write this book to men, or to the government or even the churches? Well, the simple answer is because women control the world. Men may not want to believe that, and women may not realize it, but it is true. It is no secret that whatsoever men do they do simply to either impress or appease women. And I am convinced ladies that the power God has imparted to you is the only thing that can help people to turn their hearts back once again to God and towards wanting to love.

Even when women did not have a place in political society H. W. Wiley knew that the way to get people to listen to his views on the dangers of toxic food preservatives was to appeal to the voices of women. Herbert W. Wiley saw the impact a woman's voice could have on our society and way of life at a time when women were not even allowed to vote. So, just imagine the impact a woman's voice could have on our society and way of life today.

The power of women according to God's plan can positively influence change in our world without it becoming a militarized environment. Or much, much worse, before it is subjected to destruction and devastation.

Chapter Two

I know many of you do not believe in God's love because of the state of our world. But I must emphasize the fact that God did not make the world the way it is today. We did. And we did it by not trusting in God and His word.

I am so tired of everyone blaming God for our own decisions, desires, vain imaginations, and abject hopelessness.

We are the reason there is poverty and homelessness. We are the ones that created upper, middle, and lower classes within our societies. God did not have any part in that. We are the ones that created drugs, addition, cancer, pollution, aerosol and greenhouse gasses, crime, racism, SARS, AIDS, the Coronavirus, Smallpox, the A-bomb, guns, and the list just goes on. Man has many, many inventions that God was never included in. Yet, when these inventions go wrong, or injure people, destroy families, and take lives, we blame God. And we ask why God, who is supposed to be good, allows evil things to happen? So, in order to answer this, I am going to have to ask a few questions of my own: if I give you free will but I stop you every time you wanted to do something wrong, could it still be considered free will? Or if a woman had a man who would not allow her to do certain things that she wanted to do, even if they would prove to be mistakes down the road, how would she feel about him? Would she love him? Would she resent him because he is always right? Or would she feel like he was trying to control her?

This is the same dilemma Adam faced with Eve. As human beings with a free will we do not like to be told we CAN NOT do something. Even if it is for our own good.

The scriptures say that up until the serpent, Satan, beguiled Eve in the garden, everything was perfect. 'And God saw that it was VERY good.' Genesis 1:31 (God does not make mistakes.) But how would Eve had reacted if Adam would had told her to stop? How would that one act of interfering with her free will, have affected their relationship? Is love enough to justify interfering with a person's free will if you know that person is about to make a mistake? Or to put it another way, what if Adam knew Eve was about to do something extremely stupid, like say, challenge God's word, then would it be okay for Adam to infringe upon Eve's free will? Would Eve had thanked Adam for getting involved? Or would his involvement had caused a rift in their relationship?

Would we thank God if He were always there to stop us from making foolish mistakes? Or would we want Him to just leave us alone?

This is the dilemma God contemplates when deciding whether or not to get involved in the events of our everyday lives.

There is a scripture that says before the flood 'mankind was so wicked that it repented God that he had made man on the earth.' When I read this for the first time, I thought to myself, 'Oh, Shit! God *does* make mistakes, just like we do.' But I later learned that was not what this scripture was saying. Maybe God did wonder if it would have been better to have created us without free will. But at what cost? The liberty to be able to reject God and turn our backs on His word is essential to the God/woman, God/man relationship. God wants mankind to CHOOSE to love and obey Him voluntarily. Otherwise, it would not be true love and obedience. After considering this fact I reasoned that it was not a mistake that God gave us free will, but rather, it was necessary in order for us to be autonomous and independent thinkers. We could either choose God or we could not choose God. And like so many of us today, the people of Noah's day also chose to go against God. But they did it together as one people. And even though they did not make that decision until AFTER angels came down and slept with human women, thus corrupting the human race with wickedness. God still had no choice but to destroy them because their wickedness was too overwhelming.

There is a beautiful scripture in the book of Titus that says, "They claim to know God but by their actions/deeds they deny Him." And it is true. We deny God every day. Either by the things we talk about or do not talk about; the things we do or do not do; and even by the way we dress. That is right ladies. My God even takes an interest in the way you dress. Yet, every day we tell God that we know more about ourselves and our lives than He does. Every day, we tell God that what He thinks does not matter. EVERY DAY, people find ways to tell God that His way does not work. EVERY DAY, people think they can do better than what God has already done. Or, that they can make better laws than the one's God has already established. And this sentiment gets translated into the way we deal with each other, the way we value our relationships, and the way we choose our core principles.

We have been trying to live this thing called life for so long without God but all we have done is ruined it.

[The people have lost their way, says the Lord. Go and look my daughter, go, and see that none concerns themselves with the things of the Lord. They have all gone astray to cleave to false doctrines and bask in their ungodliness.]

Maybe now is the time for us to start living our lives *With* God.

People think that being wealthy will help to change the ways of our society. They reason that if everyone were rich and had everything that made them happy the world would be a lot better. But the truth is that if we all were wealthy but did not love, we would still find reasons and excuses to be dissatisfied with our lives and the people around us. And that is a very sad reality.

Being rich only allows us to distance ourselves from one another. When we are rich, we feel like we do not need any-one or any-thing. But God wants us to lean on each other and help one another. He did not want us to be dictators of who we helped and who we did not help. But being rich enables us to do just that.

We all may not be rich but many of you have something or someone in your lives to make you happy. Yet, many of you still are not satisfied. But why is that? It is because people either do not want or do not understand the one thing that gives anyone who embraces it fulfillment. And that one thing is love.

Love is simple. Love is easy and fun. I love love. By that I mean I love the idea and principles of love. If everyone just loved one another life really would be so much easier and fulfilling.

But too often people look at love as this confusing and difficult entity. Like all it is good at is creating problems. When what we need to do is wake up and realize that we are the ones that make love problematic. We are the ones that make love difficult and confusing.

The world's concept of love is equivalent to the mechanics of a barter system. It is a 'tit for tat' or a 'what have you done for me lately' philosophy. And within this philosophical nightmare women put up with so much crap in order to prove to their men that they still love them. But this only turns God's free gift of love into something uncertain; and into something which has to constantly be reinforced and proven with gifts and gestures that I like to call 'guilt money.'

'Guilt money' comes into play when something gets done to or for someone else ostensibly without any strings attached. But farther down the road that same act gets thrown back into the recipient's face causing the recipient to guiltily acquiesce into meeting some demand or otherwise reciprocate, in one form or another. For example: I do not know many women who actually enjoy performing oral sex on their men. However, I know a lot of women who enjoy making their men happy. And they do gestures like these, and others, in hopes of prompting their men to one day do something that will make them happy in return. But this is so rife with potential disaster because the practice of trading intimacy for 'favors' within a relationship is NOT love.

Plus, if after a period of time the woman still has not been rewarded for her many 'gestures' and 'sacrifices' it will cause tension in the relationship because the woman is going to start to feel like she is being taken for granted.

But instead of simply talking this matter out candidly in order to regain power and equal footing within the relationship, women tend to lash out in retaliation by either refusing sex, bickering, and starting arguments, or by focusing exclusively on their jobs and/or children, thus being indifferent towards the needs of the relationship itself.

Women need to understand that the way to regain power in a

relationship, or any area of life, is not by being callous or careless, or by putting up walls; but rather, it is by being more caring and more transparent about what you REALLY want. It is not done by hating them that hate and disrespect you, but rather by loving them more, and being more willing to forgive them. It is not done by obsessing over what others may be saying about you, but by continuing to grow as a person *in spite of* what they might be saying.

And by grow, I do not mean to go out and achieve a bunch of accomplishments that people could praise you for. But rather, grow by getting to know who you really are. In order for us to grow we have to start by acknowledging our OWN flaws; not spend our time noticing the flaws of others.

None of this means that you have to be a doormat. But it does mean that we should never stop loving people and taking chances on them. nor should we allow other people's crap and ignorance to force us into compromising our own values and integrity.

Please ladies, stop worrying over ways to impress people who may be looking at you. Instead, you should be the one looking at you, and focusing on ways to impress yourself. Not only with regard for your appearance, but with regard for your physical, mental and spiritual wellbeing also.

It is impossible to be physically, mentally, and spiritually healthy when you are in relationships and/or friendships which exploit and take advantage of you.

Learn to be honest with yourself, about not only yourself, which is a lot harder than it sounds, but about your flaws and learned mannerisms as well. A changed behavior will silence gossip but striving to silence the one(s) gossiping will only give rise to other gossip.

By taking the time to evaluate our own depths and potential to do evil, or sin, we will be in a better position to understand not only our own sinful nature, but also the sinful nature of others.

None of us are perfect or without our own sinful issues. And the more we take the time to make an effort towards realizing that the less we would be inclined to treat one another as obsolete or expendable.

I hate it when people take the words 'nobody's perfect' and reduce them to a mantra used to excuse or defend their own behavior. Yet, these same people are the ones who readily condemn the behaviors of others.

If people really accepted that none of us are perfect, they would not be so quick to give up on each other when things got bad. They would be more forgiving and merciful. They would not throw people away and out of their lives, or into prisons to be forgotten.

People are not tools to be left hanging on a wall in the garage only to be used when a specific need arises in our lives. But yet, this is exactly the way people treat their relationships. Yeah, they are handy in a pinch, but if we had to, we have convinced ourselves and even proven, we could manage our lives without them. But this type of mentality only encourages us to look at each other's worth as less than negligible.

But the fact that none of us are perfect does not make it okay for us to abuse and take advantage of people and treat them like they are insignificant. Nor does it make it okay for others to do the same to us. But so often I have seen women allow themselves to be debased and abused because they think that love is all about making sacrifices and enduring the bad in order to get to the good. But this is a mistake.

Women need to realize that they deserve to be loved. But not because of anything they have accomplished; or because they are nice and have a good heart; or because of who they are or who they may one day become. But simply because of who God is.

Women also need to realize that love is not something that can be found through sacrifices. Love is free. It is a gift from God. And no one should be forced or tricked into earning it. Nor should anyone be deprived love because of things they have said or done in the past.

The practice of making someone earn our love or the act of taking away our love from those who disappoint or enrage us is a man made, or human concept. And this concept is contrary to the will of God.

Love is a decision. It is a conscious choice we make on a daily basis while navigating our lives. We can choose to love something or someone, and we can choose to not love something or someone. The choice is ours and ours alone. This is proven by the fact that God COMMANDED us to love our spouses and our neighbors as ourselves. If loving someone was something that we could not control or refuse to do then God would not have *instructed* us to do it.

God did not say, go hang around your friends and your neighbors and get to know them. And then, when the chemistry is right, love them. No,

God told us to love each other because He knows it is something we have the ability to CHOOSE to do.

See, if love were just some random hormonal and chemical reaction, we would not be able to say definitively that we preferred dogs over cats, or vice versa. If it were random, today we might love dogs, but tomorrow we might love birds. It would all be dependent on how our synapses and dendrites are firing and communicating from one day to the next.

Love is not some whim or impulse that sweeps us off our feet. Love is not some emotional rollercoaster. That rollercoaster feeling we experience is actually our doubts and insecurities fighting against our desires, expectations, and our need to love and be loved. We call this confusing feeling excitement. And we reason that this 'feeling' is the way our hearts tell us that we are in love. But in reality, it is our brain that ultimately decides whether to choose to love or not.

As sentient beings we just do not fall into love. We choose it. We do, however, fall into, and get swept away by ecstasy.

Ecstasy is not love.

Chapter Three

Now that I have been sentenced to a life of perpetual loneliness, every time I see a beautiful woman, I get angry with myself. This is partly because I know there are men lined up around the corners just waiting for their chance to abuse and take advantage of her, and there is not anything I can do to prevent it when she is more than willing to embrace it. And I know that most men's intentions towards women are not noble because I hear it every day from the mouths of prisoners and correction officers alike. Whenever I happen to be near these men and a women with nice lips appears on the television screen in the dayroom, or briefly comes into our housing unit, all these men talk about is how good it would feel to have those nice lips around their cocks. And it is at that moment that my fantasy of kissing her is obliterated because I know that there are women in this world who would actually suck off every guy in this dayroom and pretend like nothing happened. Or they will allow a dog who just finished licking its balls come lick their face and lips and then they will turn right around and kiss their husbands or kids right on the mouth. And if the woman who appeared on the TV or visited our unit is that kind of girl then I definitely do not want to be kissing her. But mostly I get angry because I have convinced myself that even though I am one of the few men left in this world who is still willing to appreciate and love a woman the way God intended, no woman would ever truly give a fuck about me anyway. Why would they care about a broke prisoner when they have been taught to be concerned with merely how much money I am worth, or what I can offer them other than love? Besides, anyone who browses my criminal history would quickly say that I *do not* know how to love a woman. And since I cannot prove my love from prison, I am forced to live with the mistakes I have made and with society's opinion of me.

Nevertheless, even when I see a woman who is not fortunate enough to be considered beautiful in the eyes of others, it still bothers me. And that is because I know that in order for her to get noticed over the 'beautiful' girl, she is going to have to put herself out there twice as hard, but for only a fraction of the reward.

And when I say put herself out there 'twice as hard' I literally mean more cleavage, less clothing, tighter or more revealing pants, shorts, or shirts, and by having a penchant to perform more sexual and degrading acts but with less of a liberty to say no if she starts to feel uncomfortable with the situation.

But herein lies the mettle of a woman's worth:

1) Will the abundance of attention combined with her desire to be wanted cause the glamorous woman to debase herself and abandon her morals and integrity in order to please/satisfy the depraved appetites of men? Or

2) Will the not so glamorous woman debase herself and abandon her morals and integrity in order to gain some attention and popularity? Or

3) Will both women refuse to debase themselves by maintaining their integrity even while knowing this will make them less popular, less liked, and ironically even less respected in the eyes of the people within our Godless society?

Whether a woman is glamorous or not so glamorous she undoubtedly has friends who willingly debase themselves by wearing revealing or sexually provocative clothing. But if she refuses to join her friends in flaunting themselves it will create fissures within their relationship.

No woman wants to be thought of as a slut. And especially not by one of their "prissy ass friends."

All women want to be respected, validated, and treated as equals with men. The problem is that women refuse to respect and see themselves as equals with one another.

It is hard for a woman to find a friend who supports her without having a hidden agenda. The same is true for women who are homeless or impoverished. Only these women's self-respect is already less than that of others. So how can these unfortunate women hope to find true friendship without compromising their values when they are already being subjected to degradation and disrespect; and are even scorned by members of their own gender?

However, a beautiful homeless or impoverished woman will not be homeless or impoverished, or even alone for long but at what cost?

Women think that things like money and status will elevate their self-worth. But they do not realize that the very things which are done in order to attain to these materialistic heights, are the same things which are causing them to be devalued in the eyes of those around them. And without God and an understanding of what love truly is the woman will always think she is better or more deserving than the woman next to her.

And the same principle can be applied to this whole Black Lives Matter movement. I see these people enthusiastically rallying around government buildings and monuments in order to support a common cause. They see it as a noble endeavor. It is their opportunity to contribute to the fight to change the injustices of our world. I get it. But the problem is there is no love between the individuals comprising this movement.

Therefore, after the cause has ended, whether it is successful or unsuccessful, it will only take one, just one, inter-racial incident to cause the lines of a racially biased hierarchy to be re-drawn.

Without love and understanding people are incapable of relating to one another. And if we cannot relate with each other there will be no equality. And without equality there will not be any mercy.

People talk a lot about injustice in this country. But I have noticed that it is only injustice if: 1) it happens to people we care about, know, or want to know; 2) it makes for a heart-felt headline or story; or 3) it happens to those whom society considers to be 'good people.'

Meanwhile, behind the scenes, there are people in prison serving hundred year sentences, who have no prospect of ever getting out; banks and businesses are encouraged to withhold loans and jobs from ex-cons and people with criminal histories; pedophiles and rapists who get released after serving their prison sentences are denied jobs and housing, forcing them into an impoverished existence; people of all ages (including children), are impoverished and homeless in almost every city of America; women and children are forced into sex trades due to either poverty, drug addiction, or their status as illegal immigrants. American prisoners are consistently subject to torturous conditions of confinement. All of these are injustices in the eyes of God. Yet, no one is out there protesting against them. Why? Because it is not the acceptable thing to do in the eyes of society.

Take me for an example. Let's say that when I surrendered myself to the police, the officers who arrested me beat and killed me; claiming that I tried to escape. Would society have cared that I was black and treated unjustly? Or would they only have cared about the crime(s) I allegedly committed? Would my life had mattered, or my skin color? Or only the life and skin color of the alleged victim? Does my life matter now, or the lives of all the other minorities serving disproportionate and unjust sentences? Or are we forgotten about because we were not 'good people' in the eyes of our societies?

People need to realize that ALL LIVES MATTER, not just the lives of people who are/were victims.

The bible says the Lord makes His sun to shine on the wicked and the righteous. Isn't this what love is supposed to be all about? To be fair and considerate of the needs of every person equally?

God's will was never to lock people up in prisons for the remainder of their lives. Nor is it His will that we segregate ourselves from one another due to our few dissimilarities. For we truly are more alike than we are different.

In the Black Lives Matter movement, Blacks, Puerto Ricans, along with Whites, Mexicans, Asians, and even some Jewish and Native Americans all joined together in a show of solidarity against the oppression of minorities in America.

But sadly, beneath the surface, Puerto Ricans and Blacks do not consider themselves to be brethren. And Mexicans, Jews, and Native Americans do not see each other as brethren either. Neither do the Japanese, Chinese, and Koreans consider themselves to be brethren. And not one of these minority races considers themselves to be brethren with any of the other minority races. And it is this kind of lack of unity between the minority races which is going to cause the Black Lives Matter movement to ultimately be for naught.

This is why we need God and His love. And why women need to elevate themselves so that they can cause the values and priorities of their men to be elevated as well. Otherwise, we will only continue on this vicious loop of hatred, privilege, and inequality.

Somewhere somebody suggested that laws should be created and implemented to help combat this rampant social injustice problem. But to impose a list of laws and regulations which command us to treat each other equally or else, is not going to solve the problem of people still hating and resenting one another. It may even make it worse.

Another vicious cycle of injustice that I have noticed is when people do crimes, get caught, serve time for those crimes, and get released, only to be refused housing and legal employment opportunities, which inevitably forces them to return to criminal behavior.

This is a great evil, and a new kind of racism. The definition of Double Jeopardy is to try or punish a person twice for the same crime under the same set of circumstances, which is illegal. But that is exactly what the government is doing when it encourages society to bar ex-cons from businesses and residences. This in fact is the sole purpose of the background check.

It is pointless to send a person to prison to pay for breaking the law and/or to be rehabilitated if society is encouraged to still treat that person like a criminal after he/she is released.

If society would just try to start treating prisoners and ex-prisoners like people instead of criminals, then maybe prisoners and ex-prisoners would not think crime was their only alternative.

And if judges, prosecutors, police officers, and parole or probation officers actually cared about prisoners and ex-prisoners and took an active interest in helping these people to successfully reintegrate back into society, maybe they would have half a chance at building better lives for themselves.

But instead, the laws against law breakers only get more and more stern. Therefore, the ex-prisoners take more and more aggressive measures to avoid being caught. And round and round the wheel turns as the contingency plans continue to escalate. Isn't it about time for some de-escalation? How about trying that?

Once a person has paid their debt to society by serving time in order to make amends for the laws, he/she has broken then that person should not be black balled from being provided the same opportunities which are being afforded to every other American citizen.

Or are prisoners and ex-prisoners no longer considered to be American citizens? Isn't a criminal still a person regardless of what he or she may have done in the past? Or is society just disinterested in getting to know the person that the once upon a time criminal may have grown to become?

People say the past is the past. That it is not about how many times we fall but how many times we get back up. But this is not true for the ex-criminal. In our society ex-prisoners do not get to have a comeback story. And no one is willing to stick his or her neck out to support someone who is an admitted rapist, murderer, or pedophile. Society would much rather leave these types of people locked away. Indefinitely out of sight and out of mind.

But is love, forgiveness, understanding, equality, mercy, and second chances only for good people? When God sacrificed Himself on the cross did He only do it for the good sinners? Or did He also do it for the worst of the worse, like sex traffickers, rapists, murderers, pedophiles, prostitutes and whores, racists, dictators, and people who abuse and take advantage of women and children?

Does God not love all of these? Of course, He does. And He wants all of us to love them too. He does not want us to be ostensibly polite to them while secretly hating, ridiculing, and resenting them in our hearts.

In Matthew 18:21-22 and Luke 17:4 Peter came to the Lord and asked "how oft shall my brother sin against me, and I forgive him? Till seven times?" And Jesus answered him, "if he trespasses against you seven times in a day, and seven times in a day turn again to you saying I repent; thou shalt forgive him [However], I say not unto you, until seven times; but [rather] until seventy times seven."

Isn't this conversation between Peter and Jesus exactly what giving people second, third, and fourth chances is all about? Should we not be more than willing to help people get back onto their feet after they have fallen? Or are second chances only for those people who do not commit bad crimes, and 'horrific and abominable acts'?

State of Connecticut
DIVISION OF CRIMINAL JUSTICE

OFFICE OF
THE STATE'S ATTORNEY
JUDICIAL DISTRICT OF NEW BRITAIN

BRIAN PRELESKI
STATE'S ATTORNEY

20 FRANKLIN SQUARE
NEW BRITAIN, CONNECTICUT 06051
PHONE (860) 515-5270   FAX (860) 515-5266

April 6, 2020

Leslie Williams
Inmate #250996
900 Highland Ave.
Cheshire, CT 06410

RE: Request for Sentence Modification

Dear Mr. Williams:

I am in receipt of your requested sentence modification. I'm certain that you recall that you agreed to a sentence of life without the possibility of parole to avoid a possible sentence of death. In fact, a sentence of life without the possibility of parole is the only possible sentence that can be imposed in connection with the offense of which you were convicted.

In light of this, I do not, cannot and will not agree to any modification of your sentence. Your crimes were some of the most horrific, abominable offense that I have seen in my nearly thirty years as a prosecutor.

Cordially,

Brian Preleski
State's Attorney

AN EQUAL OPPORTUNITY/AFFIRMATIVE ACTION EMPLOYER

Only by loving each other can we begin to respect one another and be willing to give people the benefit of the doubt. Without love there can be no true notion of a second chance, mercy, understanding, or forgiveness. We are all interconnected to each other. And whether we choose to embrace that reality or not, we are still all each other's people. But until we start to believe that there will be no opportunity for people with diverse races and backgrounds to ever be seen as equals in one another's eyes. Without love there can be no equality. Love is what really matters. And the only thing that matters above love is God.

JUST WORDS

PART TWO

SEX AND RELATIONSHIPS

ACCOMPANIMENT ONE

Conquered Love (together) [88 Tempo]
By Leslie Williams, Jr. a.k.a. Kleva Talent
2020 Copyright
Noted notes: 𝄾 = full rest; comma = ¼ rest; ‿ = hold for 1 beat;
- = hold for 2 beats

they thought i was dead but 𝄾
love never dies
and the more we love the more we survive 𝄾
I just, wanna talk, to you time 𝄾 𝄾 𝄾 𝄾 𝄾 𝄾 𝄾 𝄾 𝄾
I just, wanna talk, to you one time 𝄾 𝄾 𝄾 𝄾 𝄾 𝄾 𝄾 𝄾 𝄾 𝄾
the more I see her the more i'm in love 𝄾 𝄾
the more she sees me the more she can trust 𝄾 𝄾
the more we see each other
the more we get it together
there's judgements and barriers to surpass you betcha ass
just tell me if you think i'm movin' too fast 𝄾 𝄾 𝄾 𝄾 𝄾 𝄾 𝄾 𝄾 𝄾 𝄾
𝄾 𝄾 𝄾 𝄾 𝄾 𝄾 𝄾 𝄾 𝄾 𝄾 𝄾 𝄾 𝄾 𝄾 just tell me if i'm movin' too fast ‿
What is it i have to do with, thoughts of,
lovin' you huggin' you 𝄾
your physical perfection is nothin' new but i'm vexed
'cause if i can't, have you 𝄾
why should i look and be 𝄾 tantalized
and fantasize all of the day 𝄾
bap, tized in your control over me 𝄾
'cause if i didn't want you you would love me 𝄾
does that seem strange or is it just me 𝄾
doesn't that see strange o is it just me 𝄾
is it me or do you deserve better than 𝄾
dudes that confuse you you 𝄾
swear y'all in love but home he's abusin' and u sin' you? 𝄾 𝄾
are you the love he really wants? 𝄾 𝄾 𝄾
is this the love you really want? 𝄾

what's to come, when your kisses become frugal
and havin' sex, turns into nothin' more than meaningless ritual
will you get vexed and contend for love you once ♮ tas ted
or will all of the time that ya'll spent together be considered as wasted
does your love conquer ♮ does your love – conquer ♮
does your love conquer ♮ does your love – conquer ♮
does your love conquer ♮ does your love – conquer ♮
does your love conquer ♮ or will you ♮ conquer love
if I've seen it once I've seen it a thousand times
but i'm not apathetic
'cause your love's so impressive that i'm now, fascinated
but why do you tempt, my love if you don't love
my hands my face, mine eyes and mine heart ♮
behold thou are fair my love
so fair that i fear your love is a snare
oh thou fairest amongst, women ♮
'cause how is it you can love someone
who shows you no love
oh thou fairest amongst, women ♮ how fair is thy love ♭
or have you traded in your love for wine ♭
what's to come, when i can't, get you outta my mind
unconquered love is just like a drug that one imbi bes ♮
the game of love has my heart, strung up in vines ♭
besides the lady does whatever she likes, but ♮
is my love not enough,
to break down the wall that exists between us ♮ ♮
the more i see her the more i'm in love ♭ ♮
the more she sees me the more she can trust ♭ ♮
the more we see each other
the more we get it together
there's judgements and barriers to surpass
you betcha ass
just tell me if you think i'm movin' too fast

ACCOMPANIMENT ONE (PART TWO)

Platonic (together) [90 Tempo]
By Leslie Williams, Jr. a.k.a. Kleva Talent
2032 Copyright
Noted notes: 𝄽 = full rest; comma = ¼ rest; ‗ = hold for 1 beat

Educate and Elevate
people are frivolous images jumpin' off high bridges
it's sheer arrogance
that you merit mere glimpses of my Imminence' recompense
ambivalence clouds ‿your utterance then you sputter
wishin' you could circumvent the pyrotechnics of kelva
got a vendetta bludgeon what you endeavor indefinite 𝄽
infinite deficit keeps me separate from decadence
Talent's the contaminant endotox, in allergen 𝄽
Battle and murderin' them as quick as you bring 'em in 𝄽
the faster these bastards average a thousands deaths 𝄽
you gasp for a thousand breaths
if you make me pull my sword you'll get stacked wit' the rest 𝄽
i confess I'm a mess that cleaned up battin' left 𝄽 handed 𝄽
can't stand to be taken for granted 𝄽 granted i'm slanted 𝄽
the Martian has landed goddamit on Xanax I planted it
since I was rhymin' over beats by Digable Planets 𝄽
Klev will reveal your vanity never panic i candidly
Praise the Lord ‿and shit all on your fantasies 𝄽
Can't afford to Challenge me 𝄽
i will formally quell all banality
and that's just in my personal capacity,
lately I'm a sucker for love ‿casu'lly
they sayin' i'm obsessively
lettin' these pretty women get the best of me,
but mentally i'm, far from impressed 𝄽 𝄽 far from a fool 𝄾 𝄽
far from a face or a puppet on a pedestal

so they hate me 'cause clothes status and money doesn't make me
and i'm not easily led to places they wanna take me
still I'm fallin' ♮
fallin' for love wit' girls that just don't give a fuck ♮
they just wanna get a fuck and get the world fucked up on 'em
i'm on the chase for a girl that looks at life a little diff'rent
who sees the world not only how it is but how it isn't ♮
not on that pedestal ♮ not on that pedestal ♮
not on that pedestal she's, not on that pedestal
♮ ♮ ♮ ♮ ♮ ♮ ♮ ♮ ♮ ♮ ♮ ♮
Platonic ♮ ♮ ♮ ♮ ♮ Platonic

Chapter One

Dear Women,

Like I told you in the beginning of this book, some of the things that I need to say might not be things that you want to hear. But unfortunately, the men in your lives won't tell you these things because they are afraid that telling you the truth might hinder you from having sex with them.

This, however, is not a concern for me. My only concern is for you. Every woman should be loved and respected. And once women believe and accept that they will be able to understand their role in God's plan.

I've seen and heard women demand a work environment free of sexual harassment. I've seen the courts send hundreds of thousands of men and boys to jail for statutory rape. I've seen the woman's struggle for equality not only here in America, but throughout the civilizations of this world. I've seen the Me-Too movement. I've watched the commercials meant to draw attention to women suffering from rape and domestic abuse. Women collectively lobby for change every day. Change in the workplace. Change at home. Change in society. But what I don't see is women lobbying to change who they are and how they carry themselves.

And all of this has allowed me to realize that women take no responsibility for their role in contributing to the sexual harassment and abuse of girls and women. Nor are they required to. And a blatant example of this is found within our own justice system.

In most American states if a seventeen-year-old boy has sexual intercourse with his fourteen-year-old contemporary and girlfriend, the boy, by law, could be charged as a rapist. Even if the fourteen-year-old girl was the aggressor and initiated the sexual intercourse.

People try to argue that this double standard is due to the fourteen-year-old girl not being ready for a sexual relationship. However, if this same fourteen-year-old girl were to have sex with say, a fourteen- or fifteen-year-old boy, the government wouldn't say that she or he were too young for sex. In fact, it wouldn't say or do anything at all. This proves that the government isn't concerned with whether or not the fourteen-year-old girl is ready for a sexual relationship. But rather its only concern is that she doesn't engage in sexual intercourse with someone who is more than three years older than her.

Therefore, the fourteen-year-old girl gets to walk away without receiving any repercussions for her role in seducing an older person. In fact, she's free to immediately start another relationship with someone else; and to even seduce another older guy.

There has never been an incident where a younger woman was arrested or sued for trying to seduce, or otherwise seducing an older guy. It is always only older boys who are punished for succumbing to the advances of younger girls. Yet, there are no parameters set in place to protect older guys who are seduced by younger girls, when it is the older guy who is at risk of being arrested. And the fact that the older guy may have conceivably thought the younger girl was of legal age based on her appearance is not an affirmative defense in the eyes of the law.

Is that fair? Of course not. If the younger girl had just as much to lose from seducing an older guy as older guys have for succumbing to the younger girl's sexual advances, maybe younger girls would learn to be more responsible for their sexuality.

Young girls put on makeup and accessories to help make themselves look older and more attractive all the time. Then they acquire fake ID's so that they can get into clubs and parties in order to drink alcohol and PURSUE older guys. But they are never prohibited from seducing older guys by law. Nor are they punished for doing so. This has only convinced these younger women that what they're doing isn't wrong. It tells them that they can do anything they want in order to pursue a sexual relationship because only the guy is going to be punished for it.

Meanwhile, the men and young men who are victims of this deception are labeled as rapists and their lives are ruined forever. This is a great evil. And one of the reasons women and girls must learn to be responsible with their sexuality.

Another example of how women want everything to change around them, but they don't change, and aren't even asked to change, anything about themselves, is found in the workplace.

It is common knowledge that in any work environment professionalism should be expected and maintained. But professional attire doesn't mean sexy or revealing attire. It means to be professional in your overall demeanor which includes the way you dress and interact with fellow employees.

Women don't want to be sexually harassed but at the same time they are adamant about defending their RIGHTS to wear WHATEVER they want. And I agree with them to the extent that no one should put their hands or body parts on another person without the person's consent; regardless of what he or she may be wearing. However, sexual, and provocative attire is definitely a distraction and women should be more considerate and responsible for the manner in which they present themselves, especially when in a professional work environment.

When you present yourself as a sexual object then people will only see you as such. If you want people in the workplace to appreciate you for your mind and efficacy, then why are you showing off your body to them?

Your body and sexuality are special and should only be revealed to the person with whom you love and are in a relationship with.

Women tirelessly promote that they want to be respected and treated fairly despite their gender but at the same time they aren't afraid to take advantage of the opportunities their gender affords them. I mean, damn, if you know that you are only being given certain advantages and privileges because of the way you dress, or how much cleavage you show, or because of the way your ass looks in a nice pair of jeans, then why don't you get another job? Why would you WANT to stay and advance in a profession which only reward you for flaunting your sexuality? That is of course, unless you are a model, entertainer, or literally a stripper. But even these professions are all centered around rewarding women who objectify themselves. Which only encourages men to objectify them as well.

Some women argue that they dress in these ways or work these kinds of jobs because it makes them feel good about themselves. They say it gives them confidence about their body image. These women even encourage other women to flaunt their bodies and sexuality so that they too can feel empowered and confident.

One problem with this type of thinking is that it teaches women that they need to exploit themselves in order to feel good about themselves.

It teaches women that their value as women is dependent on how they look. And it subjects women to being disrespected and undervalued.

The other problem with wearing sexy or exploitive clothing is that it gives men the impression that you have little or no respect for yourselves. And a man will reason that if the woman won't respect herself then why should he respect her? Aside from that, dressing in this manner also shows that the woman has no concern for God or His word. And this is something that ungodly men find very attractive because they believe that the woman's lack of modesty and integrity means she doesn't get to demand to be treated like a woman with high standards.

But God says not to concern ourselves with whether the woman respects herself or not. We must still love her regardless because He loves her.

Women don't realize that by dressing modestly and maintaining their dignity God will reward them.

Men will find it difficult to objectify you because you aren't objectifying yourselves, and other men will defend you, then will men take you seriously. Even other women will regard you as pillars within the community, and as an example of how to conduct themselves not only before men and other women, but before God.

But without women to set the tone how will other women and young women and young girls know the difference between objectifying themselves and dignifying themselves?

You, the woman, are the key to changing your role within your societies.

You, the woman, are the key to changing the way men think about you, and the way you all think about yourselves.

You, the woman, are the key to elevating the standards of the relationship so that you are finally valued and respected the way God intended.

But you need to have a solid foundation. And that foundation *needs* to be God. If you build a relationship on just sex and laughs it is going to crumble beneath your feet. But God is a rock that will not be moved. Relying on Him will not only give you the strength to walk assuredly but also the confidence to lead other women who need help finding their way.

Otherwise, how will women know what types of jobs and clothing will honor her and the principles of her marriage or relationship; and which ones won't?

I say a woman needs to take responsibility for the role she plays in both society and her relationship because it <u>IS</u> her responsibility.

If you want to be taken seriously and respected for your job skills, then that is the image you should be promoting. Not the image of the hot co-worker in the sexy outfit that everyone wants to be around because she's so cool and all the guys can't stop staring at her.

Don't be naive by thinking that doing your job is just as important as how sexy you look while doing it. This type of thinking only proves my point that women want the harassment to stop but they still want the compliments and attention. Women need to realize that it can't be both ways. If you want the harassment to stop then you have to be willing to change the way you present yourself so that you can begin the process of helping to <u>make</u> the harassment stop.

Most women probably feel it is unfair to suggest that they change how they dress because what they wear does not have any bearing on their ability to do their jobs. But women need to realize that the workplace is an environment, and that the way they dress <u>does</u> have bearing on the way they are treated by their co-workers.

It is the same exact problem in American prisons. The government in its "wisdom" decided that prison employees cannot have sexual or even friendly relationships with prisoners. Yet, majority of the women employees, whether they be C.O.S, nurses, mental health workers, or schoolteachers, insist on coming to work wearing tight, revealing outfits, and/or formfitting uniforms and scrubs. This of course encourages the male prisoners to try to hook up with the female staff or write them letters and poems declaring their love for them; only to have the female employees respond that the male prisoners are being inappropriate.

But in reality, it is the female employees who are inappropriately harassing the male prisoners by flaunting their bodies and sexuality within a predominantly male environment where inmate-staff fraternization is prohibited.

Granted, it is a male prison so the prisoners would probably be 'hitting' on the female staff regardless of what they were wearing. And for the female employees who are dressed professionally I agree that they are just as much victims of sexual harassment as the male prisoners themselves. Nevertheless, the women employees who do flaunt themselves in a sexual manner continually refuse to acknowledge that their 'harassment' could be triggered by the way they are presenting themselves. And it is an unfair double standard for *any* woman to claim she is receiving "unwanted" attention when she insists on dressing in a manner which makes people notice her. Despite the fact she may only want "choice" individuals to notice her, and not the rabble. I am just saying.

Chapter Two

Another example of how women want change to happen around them, but they are not willing to change anything about themselves in order to help make change happen, is found within the relationship.

I hear women always complaining about how there are not any good men around. Yet, women find it empowering or liberating to walk around in public flaunting their sexuality. So when these women are being asked out on dates do you think the men are interest in them for their minds and principles? Of course not. They are attracted to these women for their *bodies*. They want sex not a relationship.

Women ague that it is not as if they are walking around naked. But they do not realize that it is EXACTLY as if they are walking around naked. A pant or shirt that hugs the shape of your breasts, nipples, ass, thighs, and vulva in public is just as revealing as being nude. But your nudity should be reserved for the man who loves you, whom you also love.

I mean, damn ladies. Is showing off your bodies and making a mockery of the sanctity of your sexuality really the only way you can attract men? Where is your modesty? No, better yet, where is your so-called CONFIDENCE? Or is your confidence merely just a product of how you feel if people tell you how good you look from one day to the next?

Please ladies, THINK! You were not created to be disrespected and abused. Nor to flaunt your sexuality to strangers.

Most of you have been taught that your bodies are your own. And that you could do with them as you please. But the truth is your body belongs to God. It is not a philosophy or some optional point of view. It is fact. And God expects you to honor Him with your bodies by respecting yourselves and each other and carrying yourselves with dignity. And also, by taking responsibility for the 'power' of your own sexuality.

It is not a mistake or accident that women are beautiful and possess the power to captivate and mesmerize men. A woman's very existence is a unique gift from God. (Genesis 2:14-21). So, of course men desire to handle and hold and caress and love you, because you are worthy of love. And the way you conduct yourselves should convey that.

Stop trying to win men's affection with sex. Sex is only supposed to be an 'expression' of the love two people feel for each other; not a tool used to make someone like you or do things for you.

God urged me to write you these things because He loves you. All of you. And since He loves you, He encouraged me to also love you. Love is free. It is FREE! Love is our strength. But it also takes strength to embrace love. Like the strength to reach out to strangers in need, or the strength to reach out in reconciliation towards those who are judging, bullying, or abandoning you and taking you for granted.

God did not command us to befriend one another but He does command us to love each other. Love is not vindictive; it does not kill someone with kindness.

Confidence is also a strength. But a different kind of strength. It is a mental strength. A strength that can only be found in knowing who you are; not in how you look or what you wear.

The sexual beauty of our bodies (both women and men) is a gift meant to be shared, but only with the person you love. To flaunt your sexual beaty in order to get attention or to advance in life is an abuse of this gift. It is selfishness and disloyalty to God. And to the person with whom you are in a relationship.

Even if you are single, your sexual beauty should remain a mystery until you find the person you want to reveal it to.

When a woman abuses her sexual beauty by flaunting it and using it to tantalize men it could cause men to become callous. They can feel slighted and even unappreciated or vengeful. I know because I was such a man. And for a man to be rejected by a woman he truly desires, only to watch her throw herself at men with money, or men who do not respect her, can turn his desire to love and be loved into an embittered resentment sustained by nothing but pain and hatred. And not just towards only the women that rejected him, but towards all women. And this is the very thing God wants to protect you from by pleading with you to maintain your modesty. God showed me that I cannot hate women for two reasons: 1) it is not your fault, and 2) He loves you so I must also love you.

My dear women, if when you want to get to know someone more personally, your go to move is to lure him with sex, it is a small wonder that your relationships fail.

Now, do not get me wrong. I am all for having sex. I mean, I am a guy. But I am just saying that to base your relationship purely on having sex is a bad idea.

How can you expect to find a good man if before you hop into bed with him the only thing you two talk about is music, movies, money, and how sexy he thinks you are?

Start being responsible with the image you are promoting of yourself. Instead of advertising that you are a great time in bed by flaunting our sexual beauty, let the way you dress and carry yourself convey that you are modest, but also open to being in a loving, respectful, and sexually fulfilling, *committed* relationship. Adhere to this knowledge and I guarantee you will start to meet a different caliber of men.

I know a lot of you are probably asking how you can be sure the men you meet are serious about being in a committed relationship. And the answer is the only way to know is to talk to him.

And I do not mean talk to him about the weather or about whether or not he likes Chinese food, but rather ask him the 'hard' questions. Instead of trying to find out if you have similar tastes or enjoy the same activities, why not ask question to find out if you are compatible with regards to God, marriage, and kids?

Maintaining a committed relationship means you are more than likely to have kids along the way. So why not find out now if that is something you both want?

The point of getting issues like this out in the open from the beginning is that it 1) shows your potential man that you are serious about maintaining the relationship with him, 2) makes it clear that you want a committed relationship so he does not have to be worried about you leaving him down the road, and 3) shows you that he probably is not serious if he does not want to discuss the types of things which are important to the maintenance of a committed relationship. Also, it gives both of you the time and opportunity to get to know each other's wants, and to weigh whether you both want to commit to the relationship or not before it becomes too serious.

Anything you could think of about yourself that may scare him away later should be discussed openly BEFORE you start having sex with him. Instead of avoiding topics that matter to you because you do not want to risk pushing him away, you should give him EVERY opportunity to run. This way if he stays you will know he is really interested in building a commitment, plus you would have already gotten the hard topics out of the way. But, if he is going to run, it would be better to let him do it early on before things have gotten too intimate, as opposed to trying to stop him from leaving you down the road after you have already given him your heart.

Tell your potential man your flaws. And encourage him to be candid with you as well so that you can show him that you are not afraid of him being honest with you. Then the two of you will have the necessary material to build a relationship on a solid foundation; and there will not be any surprises down the road.

Furthermore, this will allow the two of you to be honest with each other about what you each want in the relationship. But, if you do not really know what you want in a relationship, or better yet, what you want from a man in a relationship, then maybe you should not be having sex until you figure it out.

Knowing what you want and what each other wants will protect both of you from entering into a sexual relationship for the wrong reasons.

And this is where women are so powerful in the role that God has provided for them, but they just do not know it. Why? Well, for one, the devil does not want them to know. Therefore, he keeps you all distracted with things like beauty, weight, stature, hair color, eye color, breast size, etc., etc.

That's right ladies, the devil takes all the things that make women unique from one another and causes women to use them against themselves. What an asp, right? And the second reason that women do not realize their power is because most women just are not interest in knowing the things of God. They are too focused on matching or usurping the power of men. They want wealth and merchandise. They want security and comfortability. But most of all, they want to be happy. But even with all these things women are still so competitive they even strive to out-do one another, instead of simply learning to be content in their own successes.

And it is because of this that it is so vital that women learn not only their role in God's plan, but the man's role as well.

By getting to know Jesus Christ and the role of men and women in His plan, then will the woman truly understand her worth and power. Then will the woman be able to believe that she has no place in an abusive relationship. Then will the woman be able to believe that she does not have to display her sexual beauty in order to find or attract men. Then will the woman be able to realize that displaying her sexual beauty will only attract men who want to use and disrespect her. Then will the woman be able to perceive when a man is only interested in her for her body and not because he wants to be in a committed relationship.

I have discussed some of the wrong reasons for beginning a sexual relationship; but what are the right reasons? The answer lies in the minds and hearts of our adolescence.

See, when we are very young, we value the relationship for what it is, a bonding of a girl and boy through which we can express the way we feel about one another.

But as adults we have lived life a little, and we have demands, such as bills, children, and our careers. Therefore, we tend to seek out relationships that are easy or convenient; or ones that can help us balance the other commitments in our lives.

Hence, when the adult woman is looking for a relationship, she is only concerned about her own life and commitments. Her interest is solely in finding a man who will COMPLIMENT or FIT INTO the way she is already conducting her own lifestyle. She does not want anything in her life to change. She merely wants to incorporate the man into it. She does not see the relationship itself as having its own worth and significance. Nor does she consider the relationship in its own right to be just as important as her own lifestyle, or her children, or even her career.

On the other hand, the young girl's mind is concerned simply with the importance of having a committed relationship. Everything in the young girl's life comes second to the relationship, including her parents. The relationship is the young girl's whole world AND her life. Furthermore, she has fully embraced the concept of making the commitment towards being a "we" and no longer a "me".

Most women would read what I just wrote and then say that the young girl's perspective is a naive one. But I disagree.

The perception of the young mind, whether it be male or female, is the only perception capable of understanding the true meaning of love and its ability to maintain the committed relationship. Jesus said to come to Him with child-like faith. Why? It is because this type of faith has no limitations. It is willing to believe and trust and be openly supportive without any reservations. And without worrying about what others may say or think. But most importantly it is willing to love with no holds barred.

For instance, I am sure you all remember your first childhood crushes. And no matter how inappropriate others may have thought your obsession to be, the fact remains that had the object of your obsession, (or rather, the person you were crushing on), reciprocated those feelings in kind you would have been the happiest and most in love person in the entire universe. I know I would had been.

And I would even go as far as to say that had that person treated you right and with respect you would never have stopped loving that person. Nor would the two of you had ever broken apart. And this is the kind of love God intended for the male-female relationship.

But I am convinced that as we age, we lose this child-like faith perspective because the concern for the things of the world and for other responsibilities in our lives tends to displace our appreciation for the committed relationship. Or we simply become more and more callous or protective due to having been hurt in past relationships.

The point is that as a result of losing this child-like faith perspective women and men seek relationships for convenience not commitment.

A sexual relationship should not be abused like alcohol. Nor should it be used like a drug to help you forget your unhappiness; or to block out the things in your life which are causing you grief or stress.

The benefit of the committed relationship is that the intimacy allows you to share your stress and unhappiness with the person who loves you and won't blame you. hiding these things will only put unnecessary strain on the relationship. By being candid with your man about what you are going through it will allow him to help find a way for both of you to get through those issues together, as a team.

Beginning a sexual relationship with someone is not something that should be taken lightly. And each person should be assured that the other is truly invested in maintaining his or her side of the commitment.

The only flaw in the young person's desire to pursue a sexual relationship is that so often one is so happy just to be in the relationship that he/she does not want to risk jeopardizing it by checking if the other person is as committed as she/he hope or needs her/him to be. Such knowledge is vital to the survival of any relationship. And the lack of any commitments being established prior to sex is often the cause of many adult *and* adolescent relationships being unsuccessful.

Yes, relationships should be fun, exciting, and spontaneous. But we should also be seriously mindful about maintaining our relationships. We should not look at them as disposable aps we can swipe to the left and forget about once they have lost their pizzaz or usefulness. People need to stop looking at each other as disposable or obsolete.

If you see the person you are with as secondary to your life, then you are going to treat that person as secondary as well. And vice versa. If you and your man have not discussed committing to the relationship, then you should not be sleeping together. Make sure you both are on the same page *before* you open your legs.

Many women may argue that they cannot possibly know if they really want to be with a guy until *after* they have had sex with him. But I have loved women that I have never had sex with. And if they would have given me a chance to be with them sexually instead of rejecting me, I would have only loved them even more. See, I get that sex is an important component to maintaining a successful, committed relationship. But if all the qualities you require in a man center around him being good in bed, then you are wasting his time and your own.

I look around at all these failed marriages, and at children growing up in single-parent households and I think, 'damn, if only the parents/couple would have taken the time to plan a committed relationship instead of trying to wing it along the way, maybe they would still be together.' Or they would have been able to see early on that starting a sexual relationship would be a mistake.

Everything that is to be successful all starts with a plan. Business plan, Retirement plan, Career plan, etc. Yet, for some strange reason, people don't look at their relationships as having the same vital importance as something that has to be prepared for and planned out. Instead of just "seeing how things go" start planning your relationships. Go over the details of it with each other to make sure you both have similar goals as far as careers, a possible family, and whether you're gonna make time to raise your children or just let the nanny do it.

Also, include in your plan that you want to be with someone you love, who also loves you. Don't settle for someone who simply has financial security and/or stability, or for someone who has nothing else to offer other than an awesome body/figure. Bodies change and so do finances. True love never changes. But if you're both just simply tolerating one another, that will also eventually change, because that's not love.

Having sex is vital to COMPLETING the process of forming a bond with the other person; not to START one. Do not look at sex only as a way to relieve stress or have fun, but also you should look at it as a way to compliment or physically pay tribute to a love-based commitment.

Sex should be a giving and fulfilling experience for both people involved. Not an event in which one is only concerned about gaining something from the other person.

The problem with sexually premature relationships is that they give people the notion that sex leads to love. And therefore, that sex and love should be earned, or lavishly doled out when things are good but stingily withheld when they are not. But those are bold faced lies. Sex is just one of the things that should always remain consistent in a committed relationship. Like Paul said in Corinthians, 'if you are going to take a break from sex, do it together.' Do not leave the other person hanging and wondering what went wrong. (1 Corin. 7:5)

Love should be the foundation of your relationship. And love should also be the strength of your relationship. But sex is the jam that helps bond love and the relationship together. To turn sex into something that can be done in the absence of love is to go against the very purpose for which it was instituted by God. Yes, ladies, sex is NOT a human idea. It is a gift to us from God. And this gift between two people was intended to last for eternity. But the world has gotten away from that.

Our sexual beauty should be important to us. And also private. But in today's society women taunt saying, 'You can look, but don't touch.' This is also a great evil. Women need to realize that tantalizing men with their bodies by flaunting their nakedness directly influences the way men talk about, think about, and act towards them. Women need to take responsibility for the image they are purporting of themselves. Then maybe they will receive the respect and equality they have been deprived for so long.

But the stubborn/foolish woman says in her heart, 'I can wear what I like. Y'all do not have to look.'

But God says, 'A woman's nakedness belongs to her husband. And a man's nakedness belongs to his wife.'

Now before you start arguing that you are not married, the Word of God is clear that marriage does not happen at the ceremony, it happens when you engage in sexual intercourse and you, and your man become one flesh. Genesis 30:4. Look it up.

But yes, it is true, men do not have to look when a woman flaunts her nakedness. But she does not have to be flaunting it either. Especially if she is in a relationship with someone else.

Just like black lives, a woman's integrity matters. Do not let money and social status twist you into allowing yourselves to be used, debased, and disrespected. Stand up for your respect. Do not throw away your dignity for gaudy treasures or fleeting memories of vain moments in ecstasy.

Chapter Three

According to my observations of the relationships between women and men I have found that men have no control over their own sex lives. Women are either the ones who allow sex to happen, or they are the ones who make sex happen.

I read somewhere that people would be amazed to learn just how often sex was being had on college campuses, (pre-pandemic). When a woman wants sex, it can happen almost anywhere and at almost any moment. This is why guys are so surprised when their women alert them that the time is not now, but right now. But for the guys the difficulty with having sex has always been with getting women to give their consent.

Anyone who has ever experienced rejection can tell you that being rejected hurts. Even God, the Lord Jesus Christ cried out for relief when He was being rejected by the very people He created and loved. Yet, the world expects men to take rejection in stride. Like rejecting people and being rejected by them is something normal.

This is just proof of how little value we place on the lives and feelings of other people. Sex has become recreational, or a tool we use to help us unwind. Nothing about the male/female relationship is sacred. It has all become pointless. We even love animals more than we love each other.

But I am convinced that women can change the way the world has come to view relationships if women would simply change their role within the relationship.

Stop using sex as leverage to help you get your way. This only lessens the value of the sexual relationship and turns sex into something that should be earned or bartered.

Also, instead of dressing provocatively in order to get a guy you like to notice you, why not dress stylishly modest, like in a romper, and with some self-respect. And then just simply go up to the guy and tell him that you are interested in him. This way if he says yes, you will know he is interested in getting to know *you* and not just in getting to know your body.

Instead of allowing yourself to be impressed by the glamour of a man's image, popularity, or financial standing, who don't you look for a man who is gentle, understanding, personable, considerate, non-abusive, faithful, committed, and someone you could love who is not afraid to show and tell you that he loves you as well. Not just someone you want to hook up with because you are swept away by the excitement of the evening. Be reasonable. The excitement and drunkenness will all disappear the next day. But a commitment will last for as long as there are two people willing to commit to it.

When a woman who dresses provocatively enters a room men turn and stare at her like she is the only woman left in the world. And this is her reward. She thrives off that attention. But she does not consider the damage she causes when she rejects or dismisses the attention a man is affording her, attention which makes her feel beautiful and excited, by acting as if she is not interested in getting to know him.

There is nothing more humiliating to a man than when the woman he wants pretends to not notice how much he is into her. But ladies, just because you give a man an opportunity to learn a little more about you does not mean you are obligated to sleep with him. Whether you find that you do not like him or you do, tell him what you are feeling up front. This way there will not be any confusion, and the man will respect and appreciate you for your honesty.

But, by not telling a person exactly how you feel, or by not being clear about what you want or do not want, you risk that one date evolving into a string of unwanted advances, which can cause a woman and even a man to feel sexually harassed.

A man loves a strong assertive woman. Especially when he knows she has his best interest at heart, and that she is not being implacable just to be mean or hurtful. Women think that men are intimidated by strong, successful women, but this is a lie. Men only become insecure or intimidated by a woman's strength or success when she allows them to undermine the man's position or standing in the relationship. When a woman makes it clear to her man that her independence and/or success will never change the way she looks at him or feels for him, either by telling him, or demonstrating it to him through the way she treats him, then the man will feel more secure about his woman not wanting to abandon him.

I know that contemplating a new approach to the way you forge and maintain relationships could be scary. But it is okay. Do not let fear discourage you. fear is only a defense mechanism. And it is natural for a woman to want to protect herself from the possibility of being hurt or embarrassed. But I just want you all to learn to understand and believe that a woman's power does not come from her sexuality. A woman's power comes from God.

It is sad because most women go through life trying to avoid God, not realizing that He is the source of all their strength, patience, and resilience. Just imagine how much power these women could have if they stopped resisting God and just embrace Him. 2 Corinthians 3:5.

I know us men have failed women on so many levels, but you are not as alone as you think.

Do not let insecurity and anxiety push you into a dead-end relationship. Feeling trapped or pressured into a relationship or commitment is not love. It does not have to be like that. Love is not supposed to be hurtful or humiliating. You do not have to act tough anymore. Do not subject yourself to abuse and degradation in exchange for prestige and financial security. Starting a new path or lifestyle is going to be challenging, but you do not have to do it alone. God says that if you abide in Him, He will also abide in you.

No one should have to endure a relationship in which they have to earn the other person's love. God designed men and women to complement one another spiritually and physically. They were to be a team where both people are candidly loving towards one another. And that is exactly how a relationship should feel, like you are part of a team. A team shares the labor and the rewards equally. Whether they lose or win, they do it together. No one is singled out in neither praise nor blame.

Women and men need to learn how to love each other instead of trying to prove to ourselves that we do not need each other. Because the truth is we do need each other. And what is more is we all need God, whether we choose to believe it or not.

Now I know women do not want or like to be dependent on men. And I get that. However, at the same time women do not have a problem with causing men to be dependent on them. But I know that you are all only protecting yourselves. The way men have treated women over the centuries and even still treat women today is deplorable.

When God told Eve that Adam would rule over her, He did not mean or intend for men to try to control women. What He meant was for men to protect women and love them. but men have dropped the ball.

Therefore, I do not blame women for wanting their own money, property, and independence. Due to the way men have treated women throughout the times women have been forced into being self-sufficient, self-empowering and self-reliant. But as a result, women have also become selfish. And this needs to change if we ever hope to end discrimination and favoritism and start to see each other as one people.

Women need to know and feel that they are not alone anymore. And that can only happen if they learn to trust God's word. I know that sounds like some cheesy line in a church, but it is the truth. Men and women were not meant to be independent of God or each other. The things I am writing to you in this book will help you change the way you conduct yourselves with men and that will change the way men conduct themselves with you and one another. If women demanded better treatment and moral standards from men, the men would have no choice but to renew their minds and their ways if they want to be with you. But you women have to do it together as one, with one accord, in God, and you have to do it with faith. And then your desire will not be withheld from you. Then will there be change in this world and in the way people treat one another. And women will start to realize the power of their role in God's plan.

I remember back in the nineties Queen Latifah had this hit song entitled

'U-N-I-T-Y.' The song was about women standing up for themselves in the face of being disrespected and called profane names by men. The concept was dead on, and a needed wakeup call in our society. But it did not take because women could not unite with each other to stand up against letting themselves be put down. And this was almost thirty years ago, so you can imagine how much worse women's unity is today.

I also remember an article by Jim Crow entitled, "How To Break A Nigger Like A Mule/Horse," or something like that. I mention this article because what was deemed to be merely a hypothesis then has manifested into being all too true now.

See, women call each other 'bitches' and 'slutz' just like men call each other 'nigga'. We claim we are taking back our 'power' by divesting these nasty hurtful slurs of their negative connotations. But in reality, we have just been brain washed into using these hurtful titles against ourselves, just as Jim Crow predicted we would in that article.

The reason Queen Latifah's song did not have the morale changing effect that it should have is because morality without a moral absolute is just a relative concept. It has no power because most of us have differing opinions about what is moral and what is amoral.

This is why we need faith in God. Not faith in a religious uprising. Not faith in the concept of a higher energy. And not faith in some self-enlightened lifestyle.

People from various walks of life all talk about changing the world but they do not know how. And they do not know how because they do not know God. They do not believe that the first step to changing the world is getting to know the creator of the world. The true and living God, Jesus Christ, the Creator of the heavens, the planets, mankind, and every insect and animal. And the sustainer of them all.

See, without the Lord God, Jesus Christ everything is just relative. Our concept of what is right or wrong should not be based on our own self-fulfilling opinions. But rather, our morality should be in accord with God's word. God should be our moral compass. This is what is known as having a moral absolute. It is when something is deemed to be right or wrong not by a group of people's consensuses, but by God Himself. The ultimate authority.

But people doubt, saying, 'how could I be sure Jesus is really God?

How do I know God isn't a woman? Isn't it possible that one or all of the other belief systems are correct as well, or that what I believe is wrong?' And these are all valid questions because there is a lot of misinformation being tossed around so people have a hard time differentiating the truth from the lies.

People have accused me of being closed minded because I rely on the bible. They want me to be more open to the possibility that what God says is not actually accurate. That there can be some other explanation for the way life, the world, and the universe came to exist. They want me to call God a liar. The fact is there are way too many opinions about who God is, or if He even exists at all.

Therefore, I propose that there is really only one question which needs to be answered. And that question is, 'Who is Jesus Christ?' I think it would behoove everyone, especially you women, to take the time to sort out and uncover the truths of this man's life for five simple reasons.

1) Jesus is a living person that actually walked this earth around two thousand years ago. He is not a mythical being in some fairy tale. He is a real person just like you or me.

2) Even though there are many religions with varying beliefs, values, and doctrines, they all agree that Jesus is a true prophet of God. A true prophet is someone who speaks the word of God, or for God, and therefore she/he *does not lie*. Not once has anyone claimed that Jesus lied to them. Jesus is not a liar. Yet, people still continue to not believe in the things He says. They would rather pretend that He did not say something, or that what He did say was not literal and therefore it was taken out of context, or we just misunderstood what He really meant.

3) After Jesus was crucified and buried for three days His body vanished from within a secured and guarded tomb; just like He predicted He would, and no one has had the audacity to even pretend to claim to have found His remains. Furthermore, over 500 people saw and spoke with him AFTER He was crucified and resurrected from the dead. 1 Corinthians 15:6.

4) Jesus is the only person that said He is actually God manifested in human form. No other belief system's spokesperson ever dared to claim to be God. They all only claimed to have messages FROM God. But Jesus is the *only one* to say that He actually IS the one true and living

God. Mark 14:62.

5) And lastly, Jesus said that His death is NOT the result of any person killing Him. He even went on to say that *no person* is *ABLE* to kill Him. But that He willingly LAYS DOWN His life for the purpose of reconciling the world back to Him. John 10:14-18; 2 Corinthians 5:18; Romans 5:8-10.

Now, if these five facts are not enough to get you curious about who Jesus really is then I do not know what else to tell you. But whether you believe Jesus is God or not, there is one thing He wants us to believe and understand, and that is God still loves us. And it is this very same love which compelled Him to lay down His life for the whole world.

People hear the word love and get defensive. They start to put all kinds of qualifications and quantifiers on it because very few of them actually know what love truly is. In fact, I will go as far as saying that if a person does not know God, then it would be impossible for that person to understand love. Love, like God's word, can only be discerned spiritually. And without the Spirit of God it could not be discerned or understood. This does not mean that people will not experience love, it just means they probably will not understand it when they do experience it.

The greatest tragedy of our world today is that a majority of us do not even know who God is. Furthermore, we think that we do not need Him. We think we could be successful and live a fulfilling life without having a relationship with Him. And what is worse is that we have instilled these false beliefs and opinions into the hearts and minds of our children, AND our children's children, by forsaking to teach them the truth about God. So let's talk a little about the children.

Children are supposed to be able to look to their parents' relationship when they want to know what a loving, faithful, respectful, committed relationship looks like. Children should also be able to look to their parents to learn how to conduct themselves when the time comes for them to have relationships of their own.

The bible says, 'instruct a child in the way it should go, and the child will never depart from it.' Parents mistakenly think they are protecting their children when they shield them from the realities of life. But God does not hide reality from us. He tells us the truth so that when we do encounter the evils which permeate our reality, we will be prepared for them. And He expects us to tell our children the truth so they can be prepared as well. And them their children.

See, God, sexual relationships, and the rearing of children are all vital realities of life. It is the lack of instruction and values with regard to these three aspects of reality which has enabled societies throughout the world to be callous, indifferent, and hateful towards women and each other. And it also causes societies to encourage the disenfranchisement of non-privileged ex-prisoners, especially right here in America. It is amazing how even these two seemingly unrelated topics are so connected.

Parents make the mistake of not discussing with their children topics such as sex, homosexuality, racism, and false religion. They reason with themselves that the truth about these realities can be discovered by the child on its own. They reason that they do not want to influence their child one way or the other. But this is a huge mistake.

Take sex and homosexuality for instance. Once a man and woman reach puberty, they are capable of starting families of their own. God does not make mistakes. Yet, some argue that adolescents are not ready for sex. And some civilizations agree with them. People just love to tell God that they know better than Him. The only reason adolescents will not be ready for this aspect of their lives is if you, the parents fail to prepare them for it.

The truth is, even before they reach puberty all children are aggressively and obsessively curious about sex. And parents know this. How do I know? I know because all adults were once children. Parents just fear that if they educated their children about sex, orgasms, kissing, commitment, and the value of a sexual relationship, it may only encourage their children to start having sex. But the truth is your child may just start having sex anyway. Or she/he is probably already having sex. So wouldn't it be prudent to teach them how to properly conduct themselves in a sexual relationship?

If you fail to properly inform your children about sex and its significance to the committed relationship, they are only going to get misinformation about it from somewhere else, or from some other person. Also, if you do not establish any trust with your children with regard to sex, and other realities, by opening and maintaining a candid line of communication, they are only going to hide it from you if/when they do become sexually active. They are going to hide it if they become pregnant or get somebody pregnant. They are going to hide it when they get STI's or STD's. and finally, they are going to hide it when they start feeling sexually attracted to someone; especially if it is towards someone of the same sex.

When I was a very young boy, I had an unhealthy obsession with older women. My mom worked two to three jobs and was hardly home so I spent my time watching the Cinemax and Playboy channels on T.V. Whenever older girls and women would come to our apartment to visit my sisters or have sex with my older brother, I would always try to grab their breasts and ass checks or sneak into my brother's room while they were having sex so I could see the girls naked.

By the fourth grade I had become so out of control and emboldened that I even started to fondle my teachers at school. I was not too interest in girls my own age, but if I had found them attractive, I probably would have been groping and fondling them as well. My sexual education consisted of slasher films and any movie that showed female nudity. Everyday all I thought about was what it would feel like to finally have sex, and I had not even reached puberty yet. So I cannot even begin to imagine the thoughts and desires the children and adolescents must be struggling with today in light of the technology and lack of supervision in our morally ambiguous society. As for myself, I was so desperate in my adolescence that I would consider having sex with other boys and even animals just so I could imagine what sex with a girl might feel like. I yearned for sexual guidance but everyone I talked to thought I was too young to be feeling the way I felt. Their only advice to me was to 'wait till I was older.' And I am pretty sure that today's adults think the same way about today's youth. But they are all wrong.

Since I did not have anyone to give me a proper sexual education, I went nearly twenty-five years without realizing that groping and fondling women in order to get their attention was inappropriate. That this was not the way to let a girl know that you liked her.

Often, I would watch as guys would grope their girlfriends and even girls they had just met, and those girls did not seem to have a problem with it. Therefore, I would do it to girls I met. And when they got upset,

I just thought they were playing hard to get. But mostly I thought they were only reacting like that because they did not like me. It was ME that they did not want touching them. But thinking like that just made me angry because it made me feel like I was being excluded on purpose. Like they were all part of some conspiracy to not hook up with only me.

Children do not talk to their parents about these types of feelings and impulses because they fear they will not be taken seriously enough to be given straight forward advice. So they bottle these feelings up and try to understand them on their own. Next thing we know a young girl tries to commit suicide because the guy she is attracted to did not reciprocate. So now she feels like her life is worthless. Or a young guy forces a young girl to have sex with him because he is so in love with her, and so misguided sexually that he does not know how to control himself or explain to her how he feels about her.

But these types of impulses and reactions to being rejected do not just happen overnight. They have to be learned.

My point is that when I was born, I did not come with an insatiable desire to grope and fondle women. Just like no one exits the womb itching for an opportunity to rape someone. Nor does anyone come into the world thinking that their lives are worthless. Likewise, no one is born with the notion that they want to experience sex; let alone sex with someone of the same gender. These are all behaviors, desires, and preferences which have to be learned and cultivated over time. And that includes homosexuality, discrimination, racism, and atheism.

If you, the parent(s) are not teaching your children the truth about the realities of our world then you should be wondering from whom or from where your children are getting their information.

I guarantee you that no child comes to a conclusion about God, racism, and her or his sexual preference without first being influenced by the truth and biases of other people; especially when it comes to sex.

If you have not educated your children about sex and the value of the committed relationship by the time you are prohibiting them from having boys or girls over to the house while you are away, then you are already too late. In fact, I will be willing to wager that they have already gotten a semblance of an education about sexual relationships from somewhere or somebody else. This is a major problem because if you are not teaching your kids about sex and relationships, who is? Other kids? Pedophiles? Who is teaching your children that homosexuality is okay? Or that it is not forbidden by God? You? Other kids? Or other homosexuals?

If you trust your children with the truth and teach them to be responsible with it you may be impressed by the decisions they make, simply because you gave them the power to choose by making vital and truthful information available to them. This includes teaching them the truth about God. They say, 'Rome was not built in a day.' Well, neither are a person's values, principles, preferences, and sense of morality.

We are a civilization consumed with the symptoms generated by living our lives apart from God. We see the hate, inequality, and injustice and we think we can change it all on our own. But we do not realize that it has been trying to do things apart from God, which has caused the very symptoms we want to change.

Every day we have millions and millions of conversations. Every day we find reasons to send billions and billions of text messages and emojis. But less than .000001 percent of these conversations, texts and tweets concern the things of God. We go about our daily lives like God does not matter. We have just erased Him from our minds. I include myself in this because I was once like you, independent from God. It is time to wake up people. You are giving the devil exactly what he wants; a world full of people who hate and distrust God. People would argue that they do not hate God. But I would argue back that we either love something or someone, or we do not. If we like someone, we want to spend time with that person to learn more about that person. But if we do not like someone, we do not want that person around us. We do not even want to hear about that person. There is no middle ground. To be in the middle is to be indifferent. And indifference is just another form of hate.

If God could be placed into prison you all would have looked Him up and thrown away the key a long time ago. Not because He did anything wrong, but because you all just do not want to be bothered with Him. The world has grown accustomed to vanquishing people and things they do not like or appreciate. If God were in prison, you all would not write Him, visit Him, or sent Him money. You all would not even ask Him if He needed a conjugal visit. You all would just forget all about Him like

He did not even exist. How do I know? I know because you do it to each other. I know because you do it to me. And Jesus says when you do it to the least of His brethren then you are also doing it to Him. And even though that scripture was directed towards the Israelites in the coming kingdom, the moral lesson still applies to all of us.

Teach your children to know God. Trust them with the truth and God will reward you for it. It has been said that the children are our future, but you all have to realize that we are the future of our children. If we fail to properly educate them now, it will only result in them failing to properly educate their children down the road. And on, and on, and on. . .

Even if you the parent(s) do not believe in God you should still give your children the information they will need so that they can make an informed decision about Him for themselves. Also, tell your children the reason(s) why you do not believe in God and let them decide for themselves if your reason(s) is/are valid or not.

Chapter Four

Racism and discrimination are the hues which color the landscape of not only our society, but the landscapes of the world. Racism and discrimination are a result of us cultivating socially dysfunctional relationships. Racism is contrary to the will of God.

People forget racism and discrimination are not just American issues. Racism and discrimination also thrive in places like Spain, Puerto Rico, Brazil, Germany, Asia, Ireland, Italy, Switzerland, Mexico, Russia, Honduras, Turkey, Africa, and even Israel; just to name a few. And it is spreading more and more everyday.

But before I dig deeper into this aspect of the dysfunctional relationship, let me preface my observations by saying this: I believe it is important to clarify that all lifestyles are difficult regardless of whether we agree or disagree with the way a person chooses to live her or his life. And this includes the LGBTQ community.

Everybody desires to be loved and validated even if they do not realize it. Including those who refuse to love and validate God. Often, it is the people who do not know God who are always trying to tell others what is right and what is wrong or what is just and what is unjust. These are also the same people who cause others to feel insignificant and insecure about themselves, their body image, and their lifestyles.

When people say that in biblical times homosexuals used to be stoned to death, they often say it to show they are against homosexuality. Yet, these same people fully embrace lesbianism. They choose to overlook that lesbianism is also a form of homosexuality. In fact, it was protests spearheaded by lesbians which opened the door for gay rights, gay marriage, and homosexuals being openly accepted in society. My point is that the woman's voice has always been a powerful influencer, which can implement change.

It is no secret that God is against homosexuality, in all its forms. But God also makes it clear that He loves everyone and wants us all to be reconciled to Him, including those within the LGBTQ community. However, a lot of people think that because God is against homosexuality, it makes it okay for them to hate, disrespect, and mistreat homosexuals. But the truth is we should love them more, because not only are they struggling with their lifestyle under the scrutiny of a righteous God, but they also struggle with their lifestyle under the disapproving judgements and glares of hateful people. But this does not mean the LGBTQ lifestyle is excused in God's eyes.

In God's eyes anyone who goes against His word is a criminal. This includes but is not limited to murders, homosexuals, liars, people who worship false gods, and even people who are unfaithful in relationships. But society loves to put labels on everything, especially on our crimes and short comings. They do this so that they can try to excuse their own behavior by saying, 'well, I'm not as bad as this crime or that lifestyle, therefore, I must not really be that bad after all.' But this is a lie. In fact, God says if a person violates one law, she/he has broken the whole law.

My God is a God of mercy and a forgiver of sins. But what my God will not tolerate aside from unbelief, is a person's refusal to either acknowledge or be accountable for his/her own sin. This is what my God Jesus meant when He said that 'only the sick require a physician.' In other words, how can a physician heal someone if that person continues to deny she/he needs the physician's help?

The purpose of God's law was only to show us that we are all sinners. And it is only by acknowledging our sins that God will be allowed to forgive us. But people do not want to accept that. And the LGBTQ movement flies in the face of the truth of this principle. How can anyone be penitent about their sinful lifestyle if they are determined to boast about how proud they are to live it? For example, how can a murderer claim to be remorseful if she/he is unabashedly boasting about how happy she/he is that the person is dead?

People mistakenly believe or even teach that Sodom, Gomorrah, and the other four or five cities around them were destroyed because of their rampant homosexuality. But that is a misconception of what God was revealing to us through this tragedy. God only destroyed these cities because the people inhabiting them refused to acknowledge that the things they were doing were against His law. They refused to put faith in God's word that how they were living was wrong. And they had no shame or remorse for the fact that they were scornfully disrespecting Him so much so, God was incredulous, and He had to come down to witness it for Himself. Sound familiar? It should because that is exactly what is happening again in our world today. The only difference is that now, we are in the age of 'grace' where God is eagerly willing to forgive people for their sins through the finished work of His Son, Jesus Christ. But as Paul so aptly pointed out, we should not use the fact that God is being lenient as an excuse to do more sin plainly and shamelessly. We should not mistake God's mercy and grace for weakness.

And to even go a little deeper, a person should never use her/his sinfulness to manipulate someone else into participating in her/his sin. But this is exactly what many transgender people are doing. When a man changes his gender to female, he is not doing it to attract other transgenders or gay men, he is doing it to attract straight men. Likewise, when a woman changes her gender to male, she is not doing it to attract other transgender or gay women, she is doing it to attract straight women. Thus they are causing any straight man or straight woman who looks at them to desire them or have intercourse with them to unknowingly engage in homosexuality. This is a great evil. And often this causes many transgenders to be hated, abused, or even murdered.

Just because you are of the LGBTQ community does not mean you do not have to be responsible for your sexual beauty. Our sexuality is a very powerful medium which enables two people who love each other to strengthen the bond they have between them. It should never be flaunted recreationally or used to deceive someone. Neither should anyone be harassed or discriminated against because of their sexual preference, the color of their skin, their dependency on drugs, or their penchant to make stupid or criminal decisions. None of us are perfect. Furthermore, we all have issues and inadequacies that we struggle with. Instead of hating and singling out others because of their shortcomings, we should be more willing to love and forgive each other because we all have shortcomings of our own. And it is the fact that we share these shortcomings that should make us more relatable to one another.

But instead, people all want to be unique in one way or another. They all want to stand out from the crowd to show how different or more relevant they are than everyone around them. In order to distinguish our own plight and struggles from those of other people we have parades and throw rallies for things like Black Lives Matter, Gay Pride, Puerto Rican Pride, White Power, Women's Suffrage, Gay Rights, Greek Heritage, Irish Pride, and the list goes on and on.

We try so hard to prove that we are so different that we cannot see how much we are really so much alike in so many ways. How can we ever unite as one people if we continue to focus on ways to differentiate ourselves from one another? Instead of parades and rallies which call attention to our few differences why not throw a 'God is Real' parade? Or why not launch a 'Love is Power' rally? Or why not organize 'We All Need Each Other' marches? If we want to change this world, we are going to have to do it by changing how we view the value of those around us first.

When you see a bum on the street or hear about someone being sent to prison do you think about them as if they were part of your family, or do you tell yourself that these types of people are not significant, that it is just the way of the world? Or do you pretend to not even notice them and their predicaments?

Why is it that a person has to be rich, famous, attractive, or important before we are willing to try to identify with their humanity? Why does a person need to achieve some sort of status or accomplishment before we are willing to recognize their life as being important or relevant?

We spend so much time creating and manipulating lines that divide us. But Jesus crossed these man-made lines all the time. So much so that people in those days used to murmur against Jesus, saying things like 'how is it that He eats and drinks with publicans and sinners?' or 'can anything good come out of Nazareth?'. And so on, and so forth.

Likewise, people today do the same thing against prisoners, ex-prisoners, and the impoverished. They say things like 'you're poor, you ain't nobody!' or 'is it possible to find a good man or good woman in a prison? Or with a criminal record?' And it is views and opinions like these which enables society to look at people in these predicaments as less than people. It is the prevailing opinion within our society that people who commit 'bad' crimes are either monsters, animals, or scum. And this sentiment gets translated into the very core of our legal system. People do not want to try to relate with prisoners or ex-prisoners who have distasteful criminal backgrounds. They just want them gone. But the whole 'you don't have to kill them, but we don't want them around us' mentality is just another form of racism which promotes segregation.

It is very difficult for human beings to be honest about which punishments are just and which are extremely severe when we are being overwhelmed by our emotions. This is why God is so particular about vengeance belonging only to Him. Only God is capable of punishing us for our wrongs while at the same time loving us and showing us mercy.

Human beings in all our fallibility, are incapable of balancing the concepts of justice and forgiveness. Instead of admitting to ourselves that we are all capable of being murderers, rapists, or even homosexuals and sex traffickers, we pawn off our fears onto those who do such acts by dehumanizing them. We reason that only someone who is sub-human could do such things. Thus, making it easier for the rest of us to harass, punish, hate, and ostracize these vile people whose behavioral flaws and shortcomings ironically only makes them *more* human, not less. And more vulnerable.

This is why I do not understand how a jury can claim to be impartial or fair if they are not willing to accept or admit their own fallibility.

Meanwhile, the defendant's fate rests not on whether or not the prosecutor has proven her/his case, but rather on whether or not the jury has formed a bond with one another. Or on whether or not certain jurors would allow themselves to be pressured into siding with a verdict. Or on whether or not a juror would compromise her/his opinion just for the sake of keeping peace with other jurors who just want to go home. And to top it all off the jury is not even supervised during deliberations in order to prevent such compromises from occurring.

This is not justice. And I would argue that it should not even be lawful.

After the Amber Guyger trial people were consumed by mixed emotions over the love and mercy displayed by Botham Jean's younger brother Brandt. After Brandt hugged Amber and told her that he did not want her to go to jail, but that he forgave and loved her, the only thing the reporters could talk about was how they hoped Brandt's God driven example would touch Amber's hart and change her behavior. But the people and the reporters had failed to see that this lesson was not meant for Amber. It was meant for everybody else, but everybody missed it. God was showing us how He wants us to behave towards one another. How that even in the tragedy of death and murder we should be forgiving and loving, not spiteful and retaliatory. But everybody missed it.

As human beings we understand love from a reactive perspective. But true love, God's love, is always from a proactive perspective. Reactive love leaves openings that hatred, prejudice, envy, and covetousness can enter in through. But proactive love eliminates all of these. In order for us to stand up against hatred, racism, and discrimination we have to stand together in love. We all need to learn and experience how to start loving each other.

They say the more you see her the more you know. But I have also found that when; you start trying to get people to understand the things you have learned and experienced it really changes the way you go about living your life.

People are so adamant about having a voice and being entitled to their own opinions. But what good is a voice or an opinion, if we aren't willing to admit or accept, that our "opinions" could be wrong?

PART THREE

SIN AND HELL

ACCOMPANIMENT TWO

Pain And Glory, [90 Tempo]
By Leslie Williams, Jr. A.K.A. Kleva Talent
2004 Copyright, Revised, 2021
Noted notes: ♮ = ¼ rest, comma = 1/8 rest

<u>thirteen</u>, <u>twenty-nine</u> ‿
(snare)
power move, comin' through like a titan the beat is hot
but it's all in the writin' ♮
uneventfully managed to bind ‿ties ‿wit' the elements of
survival it's thee arri ‿val of your greatest ri ‿val <u>Castle</u>,
i had a conference wit' the daimyos of rap ♮
where i spit a thou ‿sand lyrics one track ♮
but that's impossible, got lyricists plottin', <u>Check</u>! ♮
that boy's exhor ‿bitant, watch ‿him,
they hated from east, to west coast, but they can't, stop ‿him
my gutty ♮ high ‿like ♮ Bronco's stadium
y'all ‿niggas gutty ♮ lower than, sea ‿level, just breathe ‿
niggas mad at me 'cause i fuck, she, devils wit' ease ‿
the last time i went out to pasture i might've caught me
some fleas ‿
but i'm back and mad ‿chicks on the sleeves ‿
niggas be actin' de'es ‿<u>Check</u>!
but i melt cold hearted niggas like anti freeze ‿
a prob ‿lem ♮ until the days ‿come to cease, raps, i got ‿em
If you wasn't raised ‿in these streets, best, stay out ‿'em
they ain't ready for that man ‿they ain't ready for that ♮
they ain't ready for that man ‿they ain't ready for that ♮
they ain't ready for that man ‿they ain't ready for that ♮
they ain't ready for that ♮ they ain't READY for that
this, is, who, i, was ♩♮♮♮♮♮♮♮♮♮
but that's, not, who, i, am ‿there's three, sides ‿♩
to ev'ry story my pain and glory epic epic

Grounded Mag ⌣for life ♮ Kleva Talent for that ass ⌣
pay the full price naughty niggas are never nice, nigga ♮
Check! ♮ the way my con ⌣crete slabs ⌣
pull a nigga to the curb ⌣just, like, yellow cab – Check! ♮
boy i'll side ⌣walk, scrape, that ass ⌣up ♮
don't make me stick this, gun in ya butt ♮ Check! ♮
yeah I'm back, so wha'sup your girl ⌣love the way i strut,
one, step, she dy ⌣in to give it up ♮ Check! ♮
the way I run, through her gate, like a Norseman
then skate through her ruins, like them Bruins, up in Bos ⌣ton
Mate!! ♮ ♮ yeah no accents just exclamation stamps ⌣
i asphyxiate the game ⌣like ♮ concentration camps ⌣
this beat ♮ is ti ⌣tanium rod ⌣in your cranium
i i move the crowd ⌣like panic like shots in school ⌣auditorium
watch ♮ ♮ i blow this fume ⌣in your cornea
niggas hate, to see me perform ⌣it's like dysphoria
watch, it's me ♮ my four fifth bark, is clas ⌣sic
off, the chain ⌣gang ⌣my hand ⌣game ⌣is fan ⌣tastic,
four ♭ three, two, one, you're done,
compared to my, tech, nique, boy ⌣ya style ⌣is, nun ♮
like sister Mary Clarence ♮ the act, is up ♮
put my fist, through your jaw, you better wrap, that up ♮
peep the home ⌣run, derby ♮ my, style ⌣is dirty ♮ wa ⌣ter
you get it the worst like hurricanes ⌣do Flor ⌣'da
spit, so many verse, my speech quench, the beat's, thirst ♮
so you don't try to sun ♮ i'm comin' from the east, first ♮
peep the rebirth, kid ⌣♭ i done ma ⌣stered
life, un ⌣der siege ⌣now i'm livin' life, af ⌣ter, death, ♮
took, my last ⌣breath, and held ⌣it,
had to wait like thirty years ⌣to exhale ⌣this shit,
but now i'm out of my hell ♭ ♭ and got a legacy to build ⌣
i'm a nigga from the Hill ⌣on my grind ⌣like a slave ⌣in the field ♭
i'm peace, wit' my flaws ⌣fuck your applause ⌣
and your racist ass ⌣laws ⌣
been lied on by broads ⌣like, Emmit Teal ♭
y'all know the drill ♭ and the bit ♮ and the jig, saw ⌣puzzle

the extra clips for the muzzles will
de,spond y'all niggas word back from Ka,sawn
got me like i ain't tryna give no palm to them niggas
but they might, catch, somethin' like, two, slugs for frontin'
now watch me flex, that just means i'm quick to pull somethin'
y'all like to talk a lot like y'all like to bark, and not bite
i'm, wild for life y'all niggas act, wild for one, night
all i need is one, fight, gun, knife, fist, and it's on
y'all ain't never seen it brung, like, this,
my style flip like a ba,ton
or that chick, in the club
wit' the high rise ass
lookin' like Michelle Kwan
when I grabbed that ass
fuck where her man from,
get his feelin's hurt, i'm still my grand father grand son
yeah i got that dirty water an them
i got that dirty water buffalo, stance, what!,
oh, say, can you, see by the dawn's earl y light,
the twilight's last gleamin' the crack heads still schemin'
the cop lights, still aflash
in the distance you can faintly hear the distinct, sound,
of gun, blasts
we're criminals wit' a passion to get rich or die, tryin'
you can tell by the way that the lead leave this hot, iron
we got, kids dyin' moms cryin' blood y murder
that's how it goes down in the hood when there's shots firin'
it's getting' live it's gettin' live it's gettin' live it's gettin'
live
it's getting' live in East, Haven and South, Port,
Bridge,port and Hartford got them big, courts
but Waterbury is the place i, love
'cause everywhere you go niggas thug and shed, blood
and the rich, live in places like, Sims,bury and A von
word of advice, when you gettin', robb ed stay, calm,
all my niggas got, good, hands and strong arm

so if, you don't know how to fight ♪ nigga make, bond ♪
we wild ‿for life, beneath, the class ‿es
yeah ‿i ♪ moved ‿that product but i paid ‿my tax,es ♪
my niggas role ‿up them nauticals mixed, wit' Count, Chocola,
getting' they choke, on ‿we keep the studio, burnin' ♪
spread the gos ‿pel that sixteenth vandal hit, the shelf ♪
them niggas went, hos,tile ♪
they want that energy player, i got that forty-eight, bars ‿of murder ♪
shrinin' niggas while we rhymin' in the cy,pher, fuck it
my niggas die ‿for the ducket we lifers
apple head ‿tried to rob ‿my, breth ‿ren! ♪
i'm sinnin' but i got my eye ‿on hea ‿ven ♪
yeah ‿i said i got an eye ‿on, hea ‿ven
still ‿i keep it realer than, O,prah Win,fry
'cause i know most, people don't really want me, to be, free free ♪
still ‿i keep, mindin' my toast,
'cause women wanna butter my bread ‿
they act just like, chil ‿dren ♪
they wanna try on my coats, bit if they get too, close,
they'd prob'ly try to take the kid off his post,
the General T ♪ A, V, E, L ‿K, that's Kleva T ♪ C, R, O, O, K,
and i know i can pay, to bend, rules ♪
and find ‿loopholes in a system created by greedy rac,coon[s]
but i'm broke ♪
blue ‿moon ‿bright, stars ‿life's, hard
can't tell me shit, till you spent most of your life, behind ‿bars ♪♪
and my mind's ‿been crazed ‿for days ‿
but i don't give a fuck how long i been in
i know that crime ‿still, pays ♪♪
but i also know that my rhymes ‿still ‿blaze
i love my mom but she can't accept i'm still the boy that she raised ‿
♪♪♪♪♪♪♪
i love my mom but she can't accept i'm still that boy that she raised ♪
they ain't ready for that man ‿they ain't ready for that ♪
they ain't ready for that man ‿they ain't ready for that ♪
they ain't ready for that man ‿they ain't ready for that ♪

they ain't ready for that ♮ they ain't READY for that
this, is, who, i, was ♮♮♮♮♮♮♮♮♮
but that's, not, who, i, am there's three, sides ♮
to ev'ry story my pain and glor y epic epic

JUST WORDS

Chapter One

Dear Women,

As a society we fail to teach our sons what it means to respect women. And we also fail to teach our daughters what it means to respect themselves.

Young men and women grow up thinking of sex as a pass time instead of as a medium which is vital to maintaining a stable on-going relationship. Children grow up without having the values which can only be obtained through having knowledge of God's word. And that is because the parents do not have these values themselves. Hence, our society is overrun with children raising children and none of them have any regard for moral absolutes. (They are gone astray says The Lord, they have forsaken the right way; and follow the way of Ba'laam who loved the wages of unrighteousness. 2 Peter 2:15). These are the ones who eventually rape, murder, dress provocatively, slander, bear false witness, harass, discriminate, and use sex as a means to control and manipulate their spouses in relationships. These are the ones who not only do not respect or value their own lives, but they take for granted the lives and values of others.

We the people overall have become a calloused people. When people we do not know or value die, we do not even mourn them. And when someone we do know, or value gets killed or done wrong our only response is to seek revenge. Not understanding or forgiveness, only revenge. And we call this justice, not knowing that it is really sin. And we do not know that it is sin because we do not understand the sinful nature. Nor do we want to understand it, we would much rather deny it exists.

There are a lot of myths out there about God, Satan, and heaven and hell. Some of these myths are people are mostly good in their hearts, minds, and souls; we are all children of God, born in His image; God helps those who help themselves and blesses the child who has his own, good people go to heaven, and bad people and those who commit suicide go to hell, and there are many truths and paths that will lead you to God. You just have to choose the one that is right for you personally and makes the most sense to you.

Those are all lies which I will debunk one by one throughout this chapter.

1) <u>Are people mostly good?</u>

No. People do not realize that our sinful nature makes us mostly evil. They want to believe that deep in our hearts people are essentially good. But God says, 'the heart is deceitful above all things and desperately wicked.' Random acts of kindness from our hearts does not cleanse away the evil, and smugness, and the desire to be disobedient, which the heart harbors. Only God can do that. But for argument's sake let us just say that deep in our souls we are all essentially good people. Well, if that is true, then what part of us is mostly active? What is driving us to do the things we do every day? The answer is we are driven by our selfish/evil nature. We may have our moments of doing good deeds and caring for people, but essentially our core personality is comprised of five attributes: (1) selfishness or self-preservation, (2) envy, (3) indifference towards people we do not know, and often towards people who upset us, regardless of if we know them or not, (4) covetousness or wanting what others have for ourselves, and ultimately (5) a complete disregard for God and His Word. These in a nutshell are the basic active attributes of the sinful nature.

However, people refuse to believe this because if they did, they would have to admit they are not any different than the people they want to condemn. Thinking that a person does not deserve mercy because of something that she/he has done only enables us to be indifferent and/or hateful towards that person, which all stems from our sinful/evil nature.

If you notice, the attributes of the sinful nature do not include forgiveness, mercy, or love. People would much rather be selfish than merciful or forgiving. It is just not in our nature.

The evidence shows that the nature of men and women is mostly evil. Just look at our history. We torture, beat, murder, lie/mislead/deceive, exile, isolate, harass, humiliate, ridicule, abandon, berate, starve, hang, electrocute, poison, shoot, stab, bomb, behead, burn, and even suffocate one another. And we invent more, and more ways to manifest agony and carnage every day. This is why God said we have to be born again. Our sinful nature has to be done away with, and our corrupted bodies have to be changed. Otherwise, our sinful flesh will continue to war with us and strive to rule over us.

People do not understand that even Christians are susceptible to sinning just like everybody else. Probably even more so. The only difference is that while ungodly people deny that their behavior is wrong, God-fearing people admit and acknowledge their sin and that they need help in those areas of their lives.

When a person who claims to know God dabbles in sin it does not mean that she/he has lost faith, it just means that person is struggling and could use a little help and encouragement, not criticism. Instead of saying, 'fuck that! Look at what she/he did!' we should try to be more understanding.

We are all in this war against sin together. Instead of condemning each other we should be ready to embrace those struggling with their sins and shortcomings. Isn't this what God wants? For us to love EVERYONE, and care for EVERYONE, and to uplift each other? But people are quick to criticize that which they do not understand. All they want is to condemn one another. So people developed this sort of ingrained prejudice that says: if a person does something horrible that person is no longer capable of loving someone, or that, a person that does something horrible to another person is no longer a person that could be of any benefit to society or anyone else. A perfect example of this is the woman in the bible who was caught in adultery. Society said, (I'm paraphrasing), "Stone her, it's the law, do it. She did a great wrong, she deserves to be stoned. IT'S THE LAW!!!!"

They did not see the sinful woman as having any value or significance. She had committed a horrible sin. A sin worthy of death. Therefore, in their eyes she was unredeemable. But instead of condemning her like the people wanted, God the Son forgave her. He crossed our man-made line of being implacable, unmerciful, indifferent, and divisive towards one another. Instead of pronouncing sentence on the woman He turned towards the crowd and said, (again I'm paraphrasing), "You're right, it is the law, but if any of you here has never sinned or broken any law or code of conduct, then I want you to be the one to throw the first stone."

It is no question that people are willing to accept that nowadays a former stripper, prostitute, or drug dealer could mature into a good wife or husband. But when it comes to a murderer or sex offender no one is willing to accept that these people too could change. Rather, society fights to keep people with distasteful pasts trapped in a mold which showcases their flaws. And if such a person tries to break out of that mold by bettering her/himself or getting their life in order, society rushes in to repair whatever cracks those success might have caused to the mold just so they could remind that person that she/he is no better than what society thinks of them.

I have even heard some religious leaders do the same thing. They say a person is saved AS LONG AS that person does what is right. But if that person does this or does that, then the leaders and other people question whether that person is really saved. They reason that a truly saved person would *never* conduct themselves in a sinful manner. But that is a lie. There is only one scenario in which this type of reasoning could be feasible. And that is if a person claims to believe in Jesus' death, burial, and resurrection, but after time or hardship she/he turns around and claims to no longer believe in Jesus' death, burial, and resurrection; then and only then could it be said that this person probably never believed, and thus was probably never saved to begin with. But as far as a person's behavior is concerned, it is impossible to determine a person's salvation based on the things she/he does. And to try to do so is a huge mistake. The Lord says He's the one that searches the heart, not us.

We are all sinners. It should not surprise anyone that a sinner will do sin. Being saved does not preclude a person from ever sinning again. In fact, if a person who is saved does not keep her/his eyes and nose in God's word, that person will definitely occasionally succumb to the sinful nature. But does that make her/him any less saved? Absolutely not. People try to argue that if a person were truly saved, she/he would not live in a sinful manner. But that is a lie. WE ARE SINNERS!! Being saved does not separate us from our sinful nature. However, when a person truly loves God, she/he does strive to avoid *indulging* in sinful behavior. But loving God is not a prerequisite for our salvation. There is nothing in scripture that says a person needs to LOVE God or STOP sinning in order to be saved.

Therefore, the whole argument or philosophy that says truly saved people do not do certain sins or live certain types of lifestyles is a blatant lie from the devil, meant to discourage people from embracing the love and grace of God.

Take the story of the prodigal son for example. What if after the prodigal son had squandered his fortune he got into some trouble, then defending himself he was forced to kill someone? Then, needing money he decides to rob a bank. And during all this he even manages to be accused of raping a woman. Would his father have refused to throw a feast for his son when he finally returned home? Did the son's sinful behavior cause him to no longer be his father's son? Of course not! He will always be his father's son. Just like if we are believers in Christ's work on the cross, we will always have the gift of the Holy Spirit. And nothing, not height nor depth, nor any other creature shall be able to separate us from the love of God, which is in Christ Jesus, my Lord.

People forget that Jesus died for us WHILE we were still sinners SINNING. He did not require us to get our collective acts together BEFORE He went to the cross. No. He went to the cross WHILE we were all out there indulging in our sinfulness.

Our flesh has enmity with God. It does not like Him. But us sinning is not going to make our flesh more of God's enemy than it already is. Nor by sinning are we going to undo Jesus' work on the cross. It is only our spirit which has been reborn, but our flesh is still the same. Therefore, we still have the same sinful desires warring against us. It is only through the Holy Spirit, and by loving Christ and abiding in His word will we be given the strength to resist these sinful urgings. But if we chose to not abide in Christ and His word, it does not mean we were never truly saved. It just means we need help because our sinful nature is overwhelming us.

A perfect example of this is found in the letter Paul wrote to the

Corinthians. Paul said to deliver that man to Satan for the destruction of his flesh. He did not say the destruction of his soul. That man was overwhelmed by his sinful nature. He did not want to abide in Christ. But none of that means the man was not saved. Just because a person indulges in a sinful lifestyle does not mean she/he stopped believing. It just means she/he is being overwhelmed by sinful temptations and needs help, love, and encouragement.

2)   Aren't we all children of God, made in God's image?

No. Only Adam was made in God's image. And Eve was formed out of Adam. But neither of them knew what it meant to be evil right up until the very moment they ate of the forbidden knowledge of good and evil.

After Adam and Eve received the knowledge of good and evil it was sort of like that glass shattering sound you hear on TV when a person has an aha moment or an epiphany. It is the sort of thing that once you see it, it cannot be unseen. Or in Adam and Eve's case, it was something they learned that could never be unlearned. They now knew what it meant to be naked. Thus, their consciousness was tainted with the perception of wickedness. Whereas before, they could not even imagine what wickedness looked like.

We are all children of the Adam and Eve who had their sinful natures awakened. We are not children of the Adam who was made in God's image. Therefore, before we can be called children of God, we all have to individually be reborn through God's Holy Spirit. This is why Jesus' work on the cross is so important.

See, in order for God to save us from our sinful nature, God sort of needed a 'scapegoat.' He needed someone He could blame and punish in Adam's and our places. But not only that, He also needed someone who could be tempted by the full power of the sinful nature while being strong enough to not give in to it. In other words, it had to be someone with both human and spiritual qualities. And she/he had to be able to suffer the punishment for sin, even unto death. Furthermore, this person or being could not be told to be the 'scapegoat,' she/he had to choose it voluntarily.

However, in the book of Revelations it says that none of the hosts of heaven were found worthy (or able) to be the 'scapegoat.' It does not say none were willing' it just says none were worthy (or able). No one was worthy to be able to sacrifice her/himself for the purpose of reconciling the human race back to God and saving them from destruction. Therefore, God the Son stepped forward and made Himself the 'scapegoat.' And to prevent us from ever being lost again, He seals those who believe on Him by giving them a portion of God's Holy Spirit. Causing them who believe to become part of God's family, and thereby giving them the right to be called children of the Most High God. Romans 8:15-16

But the unsaved person is not a child of God because she/he does not have the seal (or portion) of the Holy Spirit. And unsaved people do not have the seal of the Holy Spirit because they refuse to *believe* God's word that *Jesus died and is now resurrected*. Therefore, they will not be protected from the day of God's wrath.

3) <u>Does God bless those who have their own, and help those who help themselves</u>?

No. The bible is very clear that God wants us to WAIT and RELY on only Him.

It is often when we do not wait on God and go off on our own to do things for ourselves that we usually get into the most trouble. We want the rewards and opportunities that we see being afforded to other people. But everything that glitters is not gold. We have to be careful because the devil also knows how to give gifts. But each gift comes accompanied by seven trials. The grass may look greener, but it is full of things that slither, and crawl, and bite, and sting, and poison us.

The people say, 'God bless America.' But America is a country which does not have faith in God. And God says it is impossible to please Him without faith. God *cannot* bless America because she does not obey Him. People mistake America's wealth and prosperity for blessings. The people forget that the devil knows how to give gifts too. He even offered to give Jesus Himself all the kingdoms of the world if Jesus would simply worship him. And Jesus rejected his offer. But America never rejects the devil's offers. In fact, America embraces ALL of the devil's lies and philosophies.

God wants us to have things that will last and help build us up. Only Satan gives gifts that we do not need, so that he can distract us from striving to get the things that we do. Women love to emphasize focusing on ways for them to be happy. But isn't it a bit selfish for only you to be happy; while there are people around you who are miserable? It is not our job to make each other happy, but it is our job to love and care for one another. If we continue to focus on making only ourselves happy and comfortable while we are here on earth, then we will not remember that we are supposed to be on a journey, to heaven.

4) <u>If a person commits suicide, or is really, really, bad/evil, does that mean she/he will go to hell</u>?

No. People need to understand that sin is NOT what causes us to go to hell. Nobody deserves to go to hell based on anything they have done or may do. Just like nobody deserves to go to heaven because of anything they have done or may do.

I have heard people glibly say they are probably going to hell because they did this or did that. Or they even tell me about how someone committed a horrible crime, and they are convinced that person HAS to be going to hell. And I try to tell these people that is not how it works. There is no sin that anyone could do which would cause God to say that person deserves to go to hell. It is not our sins that infuriate God, it is our unbelief. Our sins have already been punished. Jesus Christ was made into sin FOR us. And God the Father punished God the Son for THREE WHOLE DAYS as our substitute and 'scapegoat'. And all God wants us to do is *Believe* that it happened.

There is only one thing that can keep a person out of heaven, and that is not believing in Jesus' death, burial, and resurrection. That's it. You may not believe that, or want to believe it, but it is true.

There is no point system. There are no tallies which have to be counted in order for you to win your salvation. And there is no working off your sins by doing good deeds in order to try to tip the scales in your favor. There is only Jesus. And it is your opinion of Him which is going to determine whether you go to hell or heaven. The choice is yours.

And yes, it is a choice, and the choice is an easy one. God made it really simple for us. He said we can either choose to believe what He says, or we can choose to not believe what He says. It is that simple. But people just cannot accept that. They say that it is 'too easy.' They say, 'but that means ANYBODY can go to heaven, rapists, rippers, sex traffickers, and even racists, and murderers.' And my response is EXACTLY!! That was the whole point of Jesus going to the cross! He wanted to make it possible for EVERYBODY to go to heaven.

And do you know what their response to that is? They say, 'it's not fair.' Can you believe that? They say Jesus is not being fair because He wants to forgive everybody. Does that make any sense to you?

See, it is people like these that Jesus will weed out from around Him. People who think they DESERVE a place in heaven and others do not. These people do not know God, otherwise they would want EVERYONE to go to heaven regardless of what sins anyone may have committed. If they knew God, they would want EVERYONE else to know and believe in Him too. They would not hope for people to go to hell. Nor would they hope for anyone to die or go to prison. But even saved people can think and desire evil things.

Are we not all supposed to want the best for each other? Isn't that what love, mercy, and forgiveness is all about? But people find it hard to be loving, forgiving, and merciful because it is not part of our nature. These things have to be taught to us by God through His Holy Spirit.

Love, mercy, and forgiveness are our greatest weapons against our sinful natures. And since God commands us to love everyone what gives anyone the right to choose whom they will or will not love?

God's invitation for salvation is to everyone. Not just to people who do not commit major crimes. We are all sinners. None of us are worth more than or less than anyone else. And the world really needs to start believing that or we will never be able to make a difference in the way we treat one another.

5) <u>Are there many truths or paths to finding God and Heaven?</u>

No. there is only one truth, one path, one God. Everything else is either philosophy, hypothesis, or just things people tell themselves to help them navigate their lives.

Having a relationship with God is not a search for some religious point of view or practice that fits into your current lifestyle. The word of God is not meant to bend to your philosophy or reasoning so that you can feel comfortable about believing in it. It is meant to expose the flaws in your philosophies and reasonings.

The word of God says to be not conformed to the ways of this world, but to rather be transformed by the renewing of your/our mind(s).

Searching for a god or religion which conforms to the way you want to live your life; on your terms is not the way to get to know God. This is what God meant when He said "and having itching ears . . . they will turn away from the truth . . ." 2 Timothy 4:3-4

The goal is not to find a belief system that sounds and feels good. The goal is to know God, because it is not knowing Him, or rather not believing He is who HE says, which is what He is going to hold against you at the Judgement.

People love to say that getting to heaven is all about our behavior or how much good we did for other people. But that is not what God says. And it is lies like this and the five I mentioned previously which causes people to never have the chance to personally know the longsuffering, compassionate, understanding, and loving God who is full of mercy, forgiveness, and the desire to reward those that diligently seek Him.

Ladies, this is why I stress the importance of you doing your own research. Take the time to learn what the bible says, and just as importantly what is does not say. And start building a relationship with God.

When I first started studying God's word, I immediately found that things people believed were in the bible just were not there. Or if they were there, they were often taken out of context.

The world has many maxims and philosophies which people would swear could be found in the bible. But they are not in the bible. They are just sayings that people made up and embellished on over the times. And people even try to use these man-made concepts and theories to challenge the wisdom of God's words. This is why women need to investigate the things I wrote in this book for themselves. Learn God's word and His values. Then people will not be able to just tell you anything and you will believe it simply because it sounds feasible or intelligent. Then, when you look around at the world, and the people, and your family, and your friends, and the things they do, and at all they talk about, and even at yourselves, you will be able to see the evidence of how far from God we have all strayed. And offer this information to your children so that they can make their own informed decisions. Let them choose to either accept or reject it, but never hide it.

JUST WORDS

POSTSCRIPT

Dear Women,

Use the revelations in this book to set in motion the catalysts that will change this world. Step up against segregation, discrimination, racism, vain competitions, ostracism, domestic abuse, the devaluing of women, and the partial and/or false education of yourselves and your children. Teach your fellow women to love each other. Teach each other the truth about God and His word. And if you do not know the truth, go find it. And help each other and all of your children to find it as well.

Teach your men and all of your sons how to love and respect all women, and also how to love and respect each other. And teach your fellow women and all of your daughters how to love and respect men and each other, and also how to stop debasing themselves for men, money, and popularity.

When your men or your sons start behaving and/or talking disrespectfully about women and/or people of other ethnicities, confront them to remind them that what they are doing is not love. And when your families and/or girlfriends start slandering other girls and/or men, and making jokes that are derogatory, discriminatory, or inflammatory, confront them to remind them that what they are doing is not love either. The scripture in James 1:26 about bridling one's tongue is not about saying 'bad' words. It is about entertaining slanderous and degrading conversations or comments. And participating in them. It is like Leah Remini said, 'the people you all are talking about probably can't hear you, [debasing them] but *you* can hear you.'

Stand up to the sexism and sexual objectification by confronting them whenever they want to make themselves seen or heard. And also by taking responsibility for the way you conduct and present yourselves. This is how you will start the process to help change the ways and mannerisms of the people in this world. It starts by reminding the people in your circle, household, and community that such behavior is not love. It is that simple.

And if these people respond by saying, 'I don't love that bitch,' or 'I don't love that rapist; faggot, pedophile; Lesbo; cracker; nigger; racist; etc., that is when you remind them that it is because of people like them, people who refuse to love EVERYONE, that the world is the way it is today. Remind them that their belligerence and hatefulness disguised as righteous anger is not a solution, but rather it is a major contributing factor to the problem.

We have to remember that even when we are angry or feeling like we are not being heard or taken seriously; or even when we think we are being taken for granted, or being disregarded, and disrespected, we can still deal with each other in love. Love is our choice. Do not let the ignorance of others divest you of your power to choose to love.

Go to the malls and the clothing stores. Go to the colleges and the hair/nail salons. Meet and reach out to the strangers in your communities and teach them to elevate themselves ABOVE the selfishness and callousness of the world through the knowledge of God's word. And watch as men who are upright and desirous of good things will be attracted to you because they need strong, knowledgeable women. Not women who are poly amorous and unsure of their self-worth, whose values do not line up with the word of God. Therefore, they are easily persuaded this way and that way by the philosophies of men and the experiences of other women who also have no knowledge of their own worth; who need to be taught how to be strong.

Why settle for little glimpses of love in one relationship here and another relationship there, when you could just take in the whole view of love in one fulfilling relationship? It is not just about knowing what you think you want, but it is also about understanding that which you are looking for, and what it is going to take in order for you to find it.

If people of this world are serious about wanting to change it, then we are all going to have to work together as one people, one race, who also are in one accord with one God. But it starts individually with you changing you, me changing me, and so on, and so forth.

Only women know how to talk to other women in a way that could get them to respond by getting involved. This is why Paul was so precise when he said that women should teach other women the word of God. But my question has always been 'but who will teach that first woman the true and sound doctrines of God's word?'

This book may or may not reach the hearts and minds of women here and there, but if the women this book touches would be moved to study God's word, *then* they will be able to use that knowledge to edify, support, and empower other women. And they would have far greater successes than, me for example, or other men trying to reach out to women ourselves. I know because throughout all my incarcerations I have been trying to reach out to women employed by the D.O.C. and/or UCONN only to be rejected. All but a couple of them thought I had an ulterior motive, and at times I did. I mean, they were hot. But I was never insincere about wanting any of them to be saved and embrace the knowledge of God's word.

But the best part about women teaching other women is that while men might find it challenging to reach women without getting distracted, for obvious reasons, women also have a knack for reaching men and getting them to respond by getting involved simply because of who women are in God's plan. And this is the power that was given to women by God. But so many of you have abused that power for the sake of self-preservation.

God gave Eve to Adam so that Adam could love and edify her. But Adam failed. Just like men have been failing to love, edify and fulfill the needs of their wives for the last six thousand years. But what are our needs? Well, the world would have us believe that we need everything other than God. That as long as we are happy and satisfied with ourselves and our lives then nothing else matters. But these are also lies. The only thing we really need is God. All the other accessories and activities that give us pleasure and excitement/entertainment are nothing more than window dressings. God will give us all of those things and much, much more.

I remember this passage in the bible where Jesus asked, 'what father would give his son a rock if he asked for bread?' It took me a lot of falling on my face in life before I was able to come to a point in my walk with God where He showed me (and I was ready to admit) that I did not trust Him. Trusting God means not relying on a back-up plan. It is when you are willing to wait on Him instead of trying to do it all on your own because you *believe* He is going to give you exactly what you asked Him for. And it is the same in any romantic relationship. If you have a man but you have other guys that you are stringing along on the sidelines, even though you may not be sleeping with them, you still are not being fully committed and trusting towards your relationship. Which is both unfair to your man and destructive for you because you are destroying your ability to trust. Which also means you are destroying your ability to love other people.

The ability to trust someone without relying on a safety net is one of loves most amazing rewards because it gives you a peace and a sense of being fulfilled within the relationship. And this allows you to have faith in your spouse's commitment to you. but only if that person is someone who is trustworthy. And that is what Jesus is talking about in that passage.

If your father is trustworthy, and you ask him for bread, you know he is going to give you what you asked for and not a rock. But I always feared that God would give me the rock, which is why despite all He has done for me I still continued to back myself into the predicament that I am now in. I could not accept that God would give someone as vile and despicable as me exactly what I needed if I would just be patient. I thought He would merely give me a substitute in place of what I asked for and not the exact thing that I wanted. I did not believe that He knew what I needed. But He does. And He knows what all of you need as well.

But, if you ask God to hook you up with that hot rich guy just because you want to show him off, abuse his money, and use him to make people jealous, then God is probably not going to hook you up with that guy. Or, if you tell God that you need a good man, but you are not a faithful and honest woman, chances are that God is not going to give you a good man until you become a better woman who knows how to treat and love a good man.

The same is true about that house you want, or that car you like, or that wardrobe you just cannot live without. God knows exactly what you need ladies. Do not let yourselves be distracted from what God is preparing for you by focusing on the things of this world.

And lastly, do not try to force your men into the role God has established for them in His plan. You have to remember that when you started the relationship you were happy with the men they are. If that has changed and you want them to elevate themselves and/or the way they value you, then ask God to open their hearts. Ask God to use your new elevated lifestyle as a means to *lovingly* encourage your men to change.

Dear women, this is your calling to be greater than entrepreneurship. Greater than a brand, an identity, and even greater than money. This is your calling to be greater than strong, beautiful mothers and wives.

Talking about God has become taboo in our communities, jobs, relationships, and even in our homes because the majority of women do not want to hear about Him. This is your calling to [help] change all that.

This is your calling to lead this world out of darkness, selfishness, indifference, self-preservation, and godlessness itself. This is your calling to greatness, not for yourselves, but for you to be great for God.

But do not try to guilt your men into becoming better men. That is not love. It has to be their choice, and it has to be one which they make voluntarily. Just be patient. Remember, behaviors cannot be learned or unlearned overnight.

And do not abandon your principles, values, and self-worth. You must remain consistent in these if you want your men and other people to start taking your role in God's plan seriously.

God bless you,
Leslie Williams, Jr. (T. J.)

POSTSCRIPT TWO

(THE HYPOTHESIS)

Premise: If you women all banded together men will not have the votes to stop you from electing the first woman president of the United States of America. This is your power. Use it to do something GREAT as opposed to using it to just get your men to take out the trash, or massage your feet, and give you oral gratification. Women outnumber men in this country by seventeen to twenty-five percent. That is a gap of seventeen to twenty-five percent in any election poll, in favor of you women.

Think about it.

TRACY AMBER KELLY

For the first time in history the United States' presidential and vice-presidential elections were won in landslides. The women's overwhelming votes outnumbering those of the men by three to one electing the nation's first women's president/vice-president tandem. And now, your president elect, Mrs. Tracy Amber Kelly.

Thank you, Mrs. Cambiandola. Hello, Ladies, (raucous applause)

Gentlemen, (applause continues). You know, when Leslie Williams, Jr. first suggested that it was women who would change the world, I thought he was feeding me some line like every other guy. You know the type ladies. I really thought he was basically just trying to get into my pants. (He was) (laughter) Yeah, obviously, right. But no. And the more I got to know him, the more I was convinced that my husband believed every word he said to me. And what is more is that I started to believe in him like he believes in me. Like he believed in all of us. (raucous applause), and look ladies, the proof, (applause continues). Here we are with not only the first female President, but the first female President, Vice-President tandem in the history of not only the country, but the history of the world (applause).

Yes. We made it. I know a lot of us dreamt but never truly believed this day would come. But it is here. Now the question is, what are we going to do with it? I will only be here four to eight years, then it is going to be someone else's turn. Preferably another woman (applause). But it cannot just be about a woman getting INTO the office. It has to be about what she does WHILE she is in here (applause). But whatever we do, we *must* do it for the right reasons (Amen, applause). See, before in our old way of thinking, we women used to tell each other 'girl, do it for yourself, this is your time, your moment, you better get yours.' But I say we cannot just do for ourselves anymore. When we only do for ourselves, we cause others to be left out. But I have learned that by doing for each other, for our husbands, and for our children we ARE actually doing for ourselves because we are teaching each other and future generations what it means to truly be a race of people who loves and supports one another, no matter what (applause).

So I say that this is NOT the time for us to be selfish, but rather this is the time for us to start showing our gratefulness to God, because He is the one who is making all of this happen. And all it cost us was a little bit of obedience to His word. This is how He is rewarding us. But it does not have to stop here. We went so long without relying on God's guidance but that has only caused us to hate and resent one another, steal from one another, and look at each other as insignificant. But now we have been given the tools and the opportunity to make all that stop (applause).

So on that note, my first order of business as Lady President is to propose a bill that will put a ban on all food eating competitions in this country. And I really hope other countries will follow suit. Food eating competitions are activities which promote selfishness, gluttony, obesity, and the waste of precious food and money which could be used to house, feed, and clothe our homeless and impoverished citizens. I will be proposing to place a temporary cap on all governmental funds being sent to aid the impoverished in foreign countries as well. How can we make a pretense of wanting to care for the homeless and impoverished abroad when we ignore the homelessness and impoverish problem we have right here in our own front yard? (raucous applause). And to aid the fight against poverty and homelessness here in America I will be proposing to start the Eradication of Poverty And Homelessness fund (applause). This project will be aided with funds from another bill I am proposing to pass, which will implement, effective immediately, a temporary, *temporary* (she laughs), do not beat me up (laughter). This bill will impose a *temporary* .001 percent poverty tax on any and all athletes, entrepreneurs, and business moguls living within the borders of the United States of America, whose net pay is nine hundred thousand dollars or more within a fiscal year. This means that if you take home seventy-five thousand dollars, or more, *per month*, this tax will require you to *temporarily* give seven hundred fifty dollars of that money to the Eradication of Poverty And Homelessness fund. And it will be non-refundable (minor grumblings). This money will be used to assist the cost of building new and improved shelters, free living facilities for the elderly, and homeless immigrants, food pantries, and soup kitchens. And also to help supply and refurbish them as well as already existing ones. America is too rich a country for its citizens to be starving and living on the streets. If any person is on the street after 12 AM it should be because that person chooses to be on the street. Not because there is no place for that person to go to get warm, a full belly, a shower, clean clothing, and a good night's sleep (applause). Also, these new food pantries, soup kitchens, and free housing facilities, and their construction will provide viable job opportunities to ex-prisoners foremost, and also to anyone else who wants to earn an honest paycheck. This is how we are going to cut down on crime. This is how we are going to end domestic violence in stressed out households. This is how we are going to decrease the recidivism rates in our communities. The answer is not to do it by creating sterner laws. The answer is to do it by loving and providing for each other. And also by opening doors for one another that would have otherwise remained closed (applause, yes, amen).

I want to implement this sort of mass-charity because I've noticed that when only individuals step up and donate to sporadic groups or causes it is always about the individual(s) doing the donating It is never about the people that actually need the help. Nor is it ever about trying to find ways to eradicate the hardships that those in need are experiencing. Instead, it becomes a sort of boastful competition of who can donate more. And that needs to stop. It should be about the ones RECEIVING the donations, not the ones donating.

I will also be looking to introduce a bill which will increase the search for and implementation of, alternative fuels and/or energy which will allow us to start healing our planet. We are not waiting any longer. We are going to do this now (raucous applause) . . .

Tracy Amber Kelly went on to serve two terms as Lady President of the United States. And America as well as the world were changed categorically as a result of her faith, strength, and leadership. And the world never needed to look back.

After Tracy Amber Kelly gave her acceptance speech, Leslie Williams, Jr. (A.K.A. Kleva Talent), performed a song which he dedicated to his wife.

The song was actually the same one he wrote about her and for her when they first started dating after she helped fight to get him released from prison.

baby girl you make me wanna flood you with atten,tion ♮
you know i wanna get into you like a pis ton ♮
i want you to put, me on like, make, up
you're the girl in my dream and i aint tryna wake, up but,
if lovin' you for one night, means losin' you from my life ♮
that's somethin' i can't, sac,rifice
the price is just, too high like debits way up in a sky ‿
wit'out limits that's why ‿
i love your hair, and your eyes shortie
and the seduc,tive way you smile for me
and the sexy way that you walk, so let's, talk
i got that poverty mark ♮ mad chinks in my armory ♮
that's why i need a girl that speaks, that minority
report, to your king with good, news you got, good sense
shortie if there was no heaven you'd be hood sent ♮
i'm like a blood, hound attracted to your good scent ♮
it's like method man said, you get that good shit
damn shortie you hot like car hoods in the summertime ‿
ev'ry time you come through the block,
it's like, sun, shine in a box ♮
i can open on rain y days ‿
i'm not like, those other dudes ‿
and the foolish games they play ♮
i just wanna love you, baby ♮ let me love you, baby,
there's no reason for you to hide me from knowin' you ♮
damn i get, so high when i approach, you
our paths would never have crossed ‿
if they weren't supposed, to ♮
don't you believe in my vision, don't you believe in trust ♮
'cause i believe God had this planned for each of us
damn baby you make, me feel ♭ so, cra zy
it's like ♮ i'm so, average but yet, so much better ♮
you're so, amorous ♮♮ so intelligent
so what if people watch,
all they'll see is us in our element ♮
let me introduce, ya ♮ this is my, world ♭

this is my fantasy ♭ this is my, girl ♭
but she's so much, more ‿than just a woman to me ♭
yes you're so much, more ‿than just a woman to me ♭
From Me To You
From Me To You, love ‿
From Me To You (Me To You)
i remember the first, rhyme ‿i read you ♭
first, time ‿i kissed you
the first, fight, we had,
was the only fight, we had ‿'cause i love you ♭
despite your dad ‿bein' a ra, cist ♭
you still, fought, to take me away, from all ‿this
'cause i'm through ♭
but i still can't, believe ‿we made ‿it ♭
through all ‿thee adversity and be ‿in' hate ‿d ♭
'cause only you believed in me when ev'ryone wouldn't
And though i changed ‿you would still be next to me if i couldn't,
And that's the shit that got me openin' my heart, to ya
    'cause if i thought you didn't love me i wouldn't have barked, but bit
    ya ♭
but i'm a man ‿that would rather ♭ walk, than hit ya ♭
anything you go, through i'm wit' ya ♭
that's why i will, never defile ‿or, beguile ‿you
nor, will i ever regret, bein' around ‿you you're all i need ♭♭
and ev'rything i want, you have ‿
from your sexy wit to your juicy ass ♭
i know it was hard ‿to try to deal wit' my, struggle wit' drugs
it was even worse to try to snuggle and hug ♭
when i smell like that ♭
my promises, pissed you off ‿it's like we're havin sex,
and we can't, get off ♭ but we fought, through,
and no matter how risky it gets, i'll never doubt, you
fuck, them drugs ‿what can be ‿more important than you ♭
in the heart of our struggle i saw your fears ‿
'cause we haven't seen, happiness in years ‿
but i'm here ‿to say ♭ i'm back, from a land ‿away,

now all we got ahead are bright ‿er days ♮ for days ‿
but we can't be getting' caught out on drugs ‿and doin' bids
    'cause when poor families fuck up that mean the state, raise ‿our, kids ‿
we gotta commit to bein' un, selfish even if life, decrees ‿
that we live, wealthless ♮
i know it seems ‿helpless, but He provides strength, in weakness
don't let the world, fool you they got what they want,
but they need ‿this ♮
we in the lead ‿right now ‿
'cause we got somethin' that's forever gonna last,
but we can never leave ‿His, path ♮
the world ‿might laugh, 'cause they can only see, my past ‿
and they won't suffer with the dreams i, have ‿
but if you, will ‿you be my blue cross ‿
i'll be your blue, shield
and we can take, charge of our life, boo ♮
From Me To You
From Me To You, [92 Tempo]
By Leslie Williams, Jr., A.K.A Kleva Talent
2010 Copywrite
Noted notes: ♮ = ¼ rest, comma = 1/8 rest

ADDITIONAL OBSERVATIONS

1) At a sentencing hearing in August 2020, the judge told Joseph DeAngelo that 'he didn't deserve any mercy' due to the severity of his crimes. But mercy is not something that a person has to earn. Mercy is giving someone leniency or a second chance despite them *not* deserving it. People just really do not know how to love and forgive one another. Some would argue, but look at what he did, look at how many lives he ruined as if the more pain he caused should reasonably justify pain being caused to him. But all these people really want is revenge.

Later in that same hearing one of the victim's family members said they wanted Mr. DeAngelo placed in the general population so that 'the other inmates can do to him what they want to do to him.' This is similar to the philosophy 'the enemy of my enemy is my friend.' Only except that society does not look at prisoners and convicts as their friends. They look at us like we are insignificant. Unless of course they want to use us to hurt other prisoners, especially prisoners like Mr. DeAngelo and myself. But what if prisoners like us successfully defended ourselves against other prisoners wanting to enforce 'society's justice,' would we be wrong? Or if we were unsuccessful would the other prisoners be right? Is society going to reward the other prisoners for harming or killing us? Of course not. In fact, regardless of what side "wins," the victors are only going to be awarded more time in prison separated from people they care about. But does society care about that? Of course not. In society's eyes the lives of prisoners and ex-prisoners are obsolete. This is why in order for black lives to matter, all lives have to matter. Because by placing distinctions or contingencies on what makes a person's life valuable, we leave room for saying that certain types of people's lives do not matter, like prisoners, rapists, and pedophiles. So if one type of person's life does not matter, then why should anyone else's?

2) People are consistently vulnerable and honest when they deal with pets and wild animals. They do not pretend to be something they are not. They do not hide who they are from animals. Yet, when people deal with other people they are especially guarded and deceptive. They do not like to let other people know what they are feeling or thinking. Particularly when they know the other person has a criminal background. Animals are abused and tortured every day but since they cannot call out for help people fall all over themselves trying to protect them. Yet, prisoners in the United States are continuously subjected to torturous and inhumane conditions of confinement and they ask for help all the time, but nobody listens. Bums and ex-cons ask people for food, jobs, shelter, and clothing every day, but people just walk right by them and pretend that their needs are not as important as say, the needs of a stray dog or an abandoned kitten. I see the infomercials pleading for nineteen dollars a month to help save battered animals, but I never see any infomercials asking to raise a dime to help the bums living on the streets. It makes me wonder if animals were capable of asking for help, would people start to ignore them?

People try to argue that animals appreciate the help more than any human would. But if you were to rescue me, or anyone, from a prison or wilderness and then gave us a place to stay or rather a place to live, and food to eat every day for the rest of our lives, I am sure we would be eternally grateful as well, anyone would. People also try to argue that animals did not do anything to warrant their mistreatment. But by the same token majority of people who commit crimes did not do anything to warrant them being born into poverty, and into being subjected to racism, the denial of jobs, privileges, and opportunities, either. Nor did they do anything to warrant them being pressured into a criminal life simply because all other doors have been barred to them. but too often society and legislators want to blame the criminal. If people really want to change the world, then when they see the injustices happening around them, they have to do something. Get involved. Do not abandon people in their need just because you think it should be somebody else's job or responsibility. I say make it YOUR responsibility too. If you can do something that will help another person in need, DO IT. Animals are created already equipped with the skills needed to enable them to survive in the wild on their own. People are not. In order for people to survive they require the help, love, and support of OTHER PEOPLE. This is what God means by love your neighbor as yourself. We are all each other's neighbors.

3) God said it is *not* good for men to be without female companionship. Even animals in captivity, shelters, and pounds are permitted to interact and mate with other animals of the opposite sex. Yet, the American government denies human prisoners the same luxury with the exception of a few states. How is this humane, or enlightened, or civilized? People just love calling God a liar.

4) Throughout history women have been the cause of much disobedience by those that love them. Adam disobeyed God for Eve. Sampson revealed the secret of his strength to Delilah, and she did not even love him back. Also, Solomon bowed to other gods in order to please women. The angels also left their assigned stations in heaven just so they could sleep with earthly women. Even David had one of his own soldiers murdered just so he could take his wife for himself. This is because women are Incredible. They are Amazing and Strong. A woman makes Everything better. When women are introduced into any venue, they increase its ambience. And this is why God created you, so that life in this world would be better. When a man looks at a woman he does not see if what she is wearing is expensive. Or if her jewelry is real or fake. He does not notice if her shoes and purse match or not, or if they are new or not. And he does not care about any of that. All he sees is her.

5) In an interview with NBCLX's Tabitha Lipkin, Jeff Foxworthy said, "it's crazy because something that a person holds onto their whole life thinking it's gonna help them retire only winds up being worth about fifty bucks. But the thing they thought was worth nothing, which they were just about to bring to the Goodwill, ends up being worth eighty THOUSAND dollars." This statement caused me to realize that the same is true about our perceptions of other people. We look at a person and all her/his accomplishments or good deeds and we think, 'wow, this is really a *great* person.' Then later we find that at home, behind closed doors this same person terrorizes her/his family. While on the flip side we see someone who gets into all sorts of trouble. However, beneath all the dirty headlines and ridicule she/he is found to be a really great friend, parent, or spouse, who only did what she/he thought to be necessary in order for her/him to survive in this selfish and callous world.

6) Today, like yesterday and the day before that, and the day before that, and the day, etc. I watched a program with an emotionally charged message. It is just odd to me that people watch these programs to get a good cry, or so that they can say things like 'wow, that movie really touched me.' Yet, their sentimentality rarely gets paid forward to any of the people they encounter every single day. They just take and take and take, but they hardly reciprocate if ever.

7) After Jacob Blake was shot seven times by police, the NBA, WNBA, MLB, Tennis players, and other sports leagues all postponed their games and matches as a way of protest against social injustice. However, the NHL refused to postpone any of their games. This is an example of what I meant when I said, 'they don't see us as brothers.' Yes, people see the injustice, but they do not look at it as if the injustice is happening to them as well as to us. They look at it like it is not happening to them at all, only to us.

8) I am a person, just like you. I am not a race. I am not a color. I am not a nationality. I am not a culture or a religion. I am not an achievement or a criminal history. And neither is anybody else.

9) Jesus Christ, Brandt Jean, and Chadwick Boseman are examples of what love looks like. It is the ability to be present, just, strong, and forgiving all at the same time. And these qualities were translated onto the screen in Black Panther when after Michael B. Jordan's character was

fatally wounded. King Tachala told him they might still be able to heal him. And Jordan's character responded, 'for what, to be locked in your prison??' but based on King Tachala's integrity and compassion for his people I am sure that like me, anyone who watched this film either said out loud or thought the unwritten line, 'It wouldn't be forever, brother.' Nevertheless, this is what mercy is supposed to look like. There is just this sort of vibe at that moment which suggested that everybody watching wanted Jordan's character to live. And that although he may have needed to go to prison it would not have been long before King Tachala would have forgiven and/or pardoned him, thus giving him a second chance. Isn't this exactly what it means to love and forgive one another? Isn't this what forgiveness looks like? Are our prisons institutions for correction, or businesses?

10) A lot of people tell God 'thank you' for various reasons, but they do not even know His name. They say, "I'll pray for you." But *who* are they praying to?

11) Confidence is a strength we all acquire by learning to know who we are, which should always start at home. Parents should not only encourage their children to be themselves, but they should ALLOW their children to be themselves. But this does not mean to leave your children to explore blindly and vulnerability. Again, give your children the core principles they will need to navigate their lives in this world. Then allow them the freedom to build on those principles and grow. Do not just assume that they will somehow discover these principles on their own. Remember, if you are not teaching them, then from whom or where are they getting their information?

12) When we claim to love someone because of traits or characteristics they possess which we find either attractive, noble, inspiring, or entertaining, it is not really love. Nor is it really love if we claim to love people because of things they have done, they do, or they either can/will do for us or even for other people. Whenever we can say we love a person because of "blank", it implies that if whatever words or phrases, we use to fill that "blank" were taken away or were no longer present we would no longer love that person. Or that if someone else came along possessing a variation of the same characteristics and traits we would also love that person. And if this is true, then our love is not.

When God chose to love us, He did not base His decision on anything we have done, or on anything we do or may do. And this is why nothing we did, do, or may do can cause Him to stop loving us. This is what true love looks like. What we consider to be love as human beings is only a flawed version of the true love God has for us and which He wants us to have for each other. These traits and characteristics which we find attractive or endearing, noble, inspirational, and entertaining are fine to use when helping us decide whether or not to be romantic with one person over another. But they should never be used to help us decide if we are going to love someone or not love someone. As human beings we have caused the words love and lust to become synonymous. In order to do this we changed the connotation of the word lust, which simply means to desire. But we reason that if we desire someone/something for the wrong reason it is lust, but if we desire someone/something for the right reason it is love; but those are lies. And it is this misunderstanding which has caused us to intertwine the meaning of true love with the notion of sexual desire. This is what led to us believing we can fall in and out of love. We have convinced ourselves that if we do not strongly desire a person sexually then we are not in love with that person. Or that if we ARE strongly desiring a person sexually then it must mean we are in love with that person. But true love is not motivated by sexuality. Sex is based purely on our physical or bodily desires. However, love is a characteristic of the Spirit. This is why it is possible to truly love someone but not be attracted to them sexually. They are two different sets of emotions, one carnal, one spiritual. But we have mistakenly fused the concepts of love and desire into one emotion. And the difference between these two concepts is one word: obedience. Loving someone means to humble ourselves to the point of being obedient to what the other person wants, even God, the Son said, "If you love me, keep my commandments." (John 14:15) also, in a love-based sexual relationship the spouses are obedient to the commandment to not commit adultery. If we are only basing our obedience on the love we have for our spouses who are fallible, then when she/he does something we dislike or disagree with it makes it easier for us to justify no longer being faithful or obedient. But if we base our obedience on the love we have for God, who is infallible, then we will have no justification for being unfaithful or disobedient. Nevertheless, the concept of sexual desire is not a form of love or obedience. Human sexual desire is solely an emotionally confusing entity which is fickle and non-committal. It has no loyalty. It has no gender. Human sexual desire is obedient to nothing other than its own gratification. This is why sexual desire absent the love needed to mold and direct it can only end in disaster and unhappiness.

13) I have seen why men are attracted to the woman. and how they are all over her, relentlessly tearing at her for their pleasure, like hounds over a bone. Only one in a thousand actually cares about her beyond that which is superficial. The rest only want to use or abuse her, or both. And when they have done so, they will throw her to the side of the road, right beside the gutters.

14) My God, the Lord Jesus Christ, is real. Our sinful nature is real. And the laws governing our salvation are resolute. Believing or adhering to a belief system which opposes or challenges the truth of God's word is not going to change God's word. God's truth is not contingent upon you agreeing with Him. Nor is your denial of Him going to change the reality of His existence. Do not let the allures within this temporal existence deceive you into squandering away your Eternal One. Just because a person refuses to acknowledge the existence of God or accept the truthfulness of who God is, and what He has done, or is doing, will not make God's existence any less a reality. Do not be misled by the notion that God is merely a product of our perception, or interpretation, or a manifestation of the conjuring of our own philosophical consciousness. We must remember that we did not create God. He created us.

15) While I was in prison, I say *was* because I do not know how long or even if I will remain after the publication of this book is complete. For if I am I allowed to choose between death and perpetual incarceration, I will choose death. Anyway, the prison guards and mental health counselors, and surprisingly even some prisoners would often stress the importance of a person finding her/his *purpose* in life. Something that makes that person want to get up every day or strive to move forward. Especially if that person's life is one of confinement. But I would always resist this philosophy, arguing that I no longer had a reason to get up or move forward because all that was important to me was now barred from ever entering into my possession, for example a wife, and freedom. This book was not written for me to find or give meaning to my life. Nor was it written for any purpose I could amplify in order to endorse the causes of others, but rather this book is the purpose of God. People strive to create purpose for themselves not realizing that God's purpose is what must and will ultimately prevail. No matter how much we resist or plan against Him. Isaiah 55: 10-11; 2 Timothy 1:9. God is far more substantive than any concept we could ever even begin to imagine.

16) Lastly, Catholics are not Christians. I was not going to include this final observation but the need for truth in our world is just too overwhelming to not include it. It is difficult for me to watch Catholics traipse around calling one another Christians because it confuses people into believing that the title Catholic and Christian are synonymous, which is a lie. The principal religion in places like Italy, Spain, and America is Catholicism. Yet, they ALL refer to themselves as Christians. The Knights of the Templar were [Roman?] CATHOLICS, not Christians. When someone hears or thinks about the inquisition, they immediately associate that word with Christians. They do not realize that it was *Catholics* who carried out those atrocities. In fact, Christians themselves were actually victims to those same atrocities in China, Italy, and even right here in America because they refused to abandon their faith as Christians in order to be converted to Catholicism. But a lot of them did convert in droves. They reasoned that converting would not be too bad because they would still retain the title, Christian. However, the practice of the religion they were adopting was wholly Catholic. Do your research. Meanwhile, here are two fool proof ways to differentiate Catholics from Christians. 1) God says to not create any graven image of anyone or anything in heaven above or the earth below to worship them, Exodus 20: 4-5. Yet, Catholics create graven images of Jesus, Mary, the so called "saints", and various others in DIRECT opposition to what God commands. 2) God says to NOT call any man Father, Matt. 23:9; And, that there is only *ONE* mediator between God and mankind and only one name by which *EVERYONE* must be saved, 1 Timothy 2:5; Acts 4:12. Yet, Catholics appoint men as priests or (fathers), and women as nuns to "bless" people and forgive sins while calling on the strength, protection, and guidance of so called Saints who have died, and offering prayers to *Mary* in the hope that she will make intercession with Jesus on behalf of those who are religious, because they believe that being religious and being righteous are the same thing, but that's a lie. Catholics also teach that unless a person is baptized and confesses her/his sins regularly to a priest/Father for absolution she/he will not be forgiven or saved. All of these Catholic practices are completely contradictory to what is taught in the pages of the Holy Bible. Yet, Catholics continue to call themselves Christians and brandish a version of the Holy Bible while failing to adhere to any of its precepts. Instead, Catholics create and practice their own man-made laws, doctrines, and traditions. Do your research.

17) But before I forget: Another thing I observed is that people love choices which they consider to be the safest. They do not want to have an employee, friend, or co-worker who has a criminal record. Nor do they want a lover who has been emotionally "scarred or damaged" by their past or a hurtful relationship. But would it not be safer and or more prudent to choose the person with the unpleasant past? The person who has been to prison, or hell and back and therefore knows that she/he has no desire to return? Because the person who has not experienced such things tends to take those types of experiences for granted. They are careless because they do not know what it is like to lose their freedom or to be abused and manipulated by someone they trusted. But do not choose the person who has been made callous by their experiences. Rather, choose the one who has learned from them and wants to do what is right. Or choose the one who has grown from them and has come to truly appreciate a loving and committed relationship. For the one who has learned from loss and or pain does not take anything for granted anymore because they have experienced what it is like to be on the other side.

AUTHOR'S NOTE

This book is very limited with regard to the amount of scriptural references I used to illustrate some of my points. I could have incorporated a lot more scripture, but I did not want this to be that kind of a book. The rhymes or lyrical verse I included in this work because each one has an aspect or some insight about myself that I felt needed to be shared with you, the reader. I apologize for forcing you to suffer through the entirety of each rhyme or poem just so I could make a small statement or observation that I probably could have made in a different way. I just felt this was way simpler.

I have been playing the trumpet and reading sheet music since I was nine years old. When I was ten, I wrote a ballad called 'Open Your Eyes.' It was for a girl I had a crush on at school who kept pretending she did not know that I liked her. I was intending to sing it to her, but I never did. I ended up writing her a note instead, which of course she rejected by throwing it in the garbage pail. Then later that day we got in an argument. Afterward, I wrote her another note, cussing her out.

When that day was over, I started skipping school a lot. I just could not deal with being around her.

At home my brother Kason and his friends would go into the backroom of our apartment where they would blast the volume on the music they were making. I would counter by blasting Rock & Roll songs on the TV set in the living room. When I was 13 and a half I started smoking weed and hanging out with older crowds. My brother told me that if I wanted to hang out with him, I had to write a rhyme first, so I wrote my first rap. And apparently it was not too bad because my brother started showing me how to work the equipment in his makeshift studio.

By the time I turned nineteen I had already written over 20 songs and had collaborations with various young startup groups and veterans throughout the city of Waterbury. This included groups like KRAZE Kids, The GRIP, Future Demand, B.O.S., E-Lo, 2 For Da Trouble, Y. B., The L. O. D., and the Diamond Brothers, a duo, which was comprised of myself and my boy Sweet, AKA Infinity/Forever. Also the Brick Posse.

I say we 'manufacture' music because none of us really knew anything about how to seriously get produced or noticed without having any money. It was not like it is today where people have the Internet, and they can post a song and possibly go viral overnight. All we did back then was rhyme at parties or battles, make track tapes, and send demos to people who had made it big, hoping they would get back to us. But no one ever did. Still we continue to manufacture a lot of music. Including collaborations I did with my brother, and classics like Challenge; Just like Dis; Gift From Da Devil; Life Under Siege; One Two Three; Killa Raw Connect; Da Octagon; Ya Wan Romp?, From Me To You; The Flower Plot; It Doesn't Have To Be Like That; Tempt Da Lord; All The Time; (but I like Drake's version much more better than the one I wrote twenty-eight years ago); Put Ya Hands Up; Thinking Of Rap; We Tend To Think Of Violence; Knowledge OF Madness; and more I cannot remember.

Yeah, it is safe to say we 'manufactured' a lot of music. But most of those track tapes and demos have either been lost or destroyed over the years. See, my brother Kason, was the one who kept most of the music equipment, but since he was always going back and forth to jail, or always getting caught cheating on his girlfriends, a lot of his property/tapes either got discarded or broken, which would include some of my own music as well.

When I turned nineteen, three years after I wrote 'Just Like Dis,' I went to prison as well for burglary. While I was inside, I picked up the Bible for the first time in my life and God started to teach me the truth of his word. I served ten months out of a one-year sentence. I T.S.'ed out twice.

In 1998, when I was twenty-two, I went to prison again, only that time it was for a rape that I not only did not do, but the rape itself never even actually happened. Yet, I still had to do nine and one-half years for that shit because I was afraid to take it to trial and put my life in the hands of a biased/prejudiced jury and a corrupt American justice system. So for nine and one-half years I wrote my music and studied my Bible.

By the time I was released in 2008 I had completed what I thought would be my debut work, entitled 'The Sixteenth Vandal.' Plus, I had enough material leftover for possible sophomore and junior projects as well.

But when I hit the streets of the real world, I found that the same false accusations from nine and one-half years before were still causing me to be ostracized, denied jobs/housing, and disenfranchised by not only society, but also by members of my own family. What is worse is that all the music I had written would once again be lost three weeks after I was released due to me being re-arrested for the terrible crimes which would ultimately result in me receiving the natural life sentence I am currently serving.

It is ironic because after I got arrested, I learned that on the day prior to my arrest my family had been looking for me so that they could tell me they had worked out a way for me to have a place to stay until I was able to get onto my feet. But since I did not have money to buy minutes for my phone, I was not able to get any of the calls.

I guess the takeaway is this, when a person comes to you for help, and it is in your power to do so, help her/him. Because you can never know what the pressure of her/his predicament may cause her/him to do; we all need each other.

Hence, most of the music I am investing into this book is either things I have recently written, or fragments from older material which I managed to dredge up from memory. I am adding the music because it is part of who I am. And this book would not be complete without it.

I have realized for some time that my perceptions about God in 'Just Like Dis' are all wrong. But it is still a good song. Plus, it shows where I was at in my state of mind then, and how much I have grown in the knowledge of Christ since then. Also, the beat that my brother made for me to drop/lay it on is just killer: titanium. I really hope there are dubbed copies of this song and my other works still floating around out there so that you all could have the chance to hear them and hear me. But that particular song, with that particular beat just gets people to stop and think about what is really going on in this world. And that's exactly what I was going for when I wrote it.

EPILOGUE

Just Like Diss, [88 Tempo]
By Leslie Williams, Jr., A.K.A. Kleva Talent
1992 Copyright
Noted notes: ♮ = ¼ rest, comma = 1/8 rest

why the fuck am i here ♮
to shed tears ‿and thank that nigga Je ‿sus,
hopin' that that nigga come and save, us
He threw us to the center of the dust ♮
i freak but i must, declare ♮
why the fuck the Klev is here ♮
it started on the day i was born ‿i was sworn ‿
to push, seventy years ‿of black, misery they killin me
they brought me to this city ♮ raised ‿me ♮
to be a lovin' ba ‿by but i grew up out, of all that sanity
what's my fuckin' purpose ♮ am i trapped in God's ‿deadly cir‿cus ♮
beggin' for forgiveness on a case, that's help,less ♮
is it a shame ‿to wonder why i gots to die ‿one day,

when i survived so many ways ♭
i wish i had a refund ♭ or everlastin' reruns ♭
the bible's good to learn from ♭ but none is half the real one
and this is how i feel Son ♭
you bled from three points, and then you gave us joints
to toke from, the deadly web was ♭ spun ♭
'cause [now] the white man has guided his plan ‿
To run the black, man got a million deputized to stand ♭
i'm tired as hell man reality's a joke ♭
got ev'ry nigga tokin' ♭ got ev'ry nigga sellin' coke
the secret to this, joke, is not to play the game ‿
but it's hard to maintain ♭
when you're ridin' on a non-stop train ♭
that be brake,less, speedin' up to diff'rent rac,es
a hundred paces of death, and mad cases,
mad fuckin' vicious ♭ i'm kickin' physics ♭
rippin wicked on some shit that we can't fuck, wit',
Just Like Diss, there ain't no sit back, relax, 'in this world's ama zin'
Got me caught up in this fucked up destruction, seduction,
Like i'm really livin' somethin' so great,
i'm tryin' to lounge but God be poundin' on my chest, plate ♭
so now you know why ♭ there's no way, to strive wit' this,
i play the black side so more tribes can rise wit' this,
then we all can slide, to a fucked life, of happiness ♭
i'm wonderin' why ♭ do this world gots to be like, this
(like this, like this, like this)
one two one two what you got,ta say ♭♭ hey ‿
one two one two what you got,ta say ♭♭ hey ‿
Just like Diss ♭ why like this ♭
Just like Diss ♭ why like this ♭
Just like Diss ♭ why like this ♭
Just like Diss (like Diss, like Diss)

REFERENCES

Recommended Reading/Study Material:
Through The Bible, by Les Feldick. This man is blessed with the ability to make the Bible clearer to both novices and scholars. Do your research. Also, anything by Dr. Peter S. Ruckman, and Dr. Peter P. Ventura.

1. Ecclesiastes 7:21
2. Genesis 6:6
3. Genesis 6:5-8
4. Genesis 6:1-7
5. Titus 1:16
6. Matthew 19:19; Ephesians 5:28
7. Matthew 5:44-47
8. Hebrews 11:6; Psalms 19:7-11; 1 Timothy 5:18
9. Galatians 5:14
10. Luke 18:17
11. 1 Corinthians 7:4
12. John 15:4-5
13. Colossians 1:16-17; John 1:1-3
14. John 6:14; Matthew 21:11
15. Isaiah 53:9; 1 Peter 2:22
16. 1 Corinthians 2:14; Galatians 5:22-23
17. Proverbs 22:6
18. 1 Corinthians 7:36
19. Matthew 25:41-45
20. Deuteronomy 11:28
21. Romans 1:26-27
22. John 3:16-17
23. Exodus 20:1-7
24. James 2:10; Galatians 3:10
25. Luke 5:31
26. Hebrews 10:1-4; Romans 3:19-20
27. Psalms 32:5; 1 Johns 1:8-10
28. Genesis 18:20-21; Romans 1:26-32

29. Romans 6:15; Galatians 5:13
30. Ephesians 1:13
31. Jeremiah 17:9
32. 1 Peter 1:23
33. 1 Corinthians 15:50-58
34. John 8:3-11
35. Jeremiah 9:10
36. Romans 8:38
37. Ephesians 2:15-16; James 4:4; Romans 8:7-9
38. 1 Peter 3:18; Ephesians 2:1-6
39. 1 Corinthians 5:5
40. Revelations 5:4-9
41. 1 Timothy 5:18; Psalms 19:7-11; Deuteronomy 11:28
42. Matthew 4:8-9
43. Hebrews 11:6; Numbers 14:11-12, 20-23
44. 2 Corinthians 5:21
45. Matthew 12:40; Mark 8:31; Acts 3:18
46. Matthew 12:31
47. Matthew 25:41-45
48. Romans 12:2
49. Matthew 7:21-23
50. Exodus 33:19; Jeremiah 9:24; Hebrews 11:6
51. Proverbs 16:6
52. Hebrews 11:6
53. Matthew 7:9-11
54. Galatians 5:14
55. Genesis 2:18
56. Genesis 2:18

ABOUT THE AUTHOR

Dear Reader,

I just want to say I hope you got everything out of this book that I intended. I encourage anyone with questions to please do your research. Do not just accept one person's point of view because she/he has a degree or certificate. If Paul were alive in our society, he would be considered a heretic, just as he was back then. Yet, he was given revelation directly from God. Himself.

You could write me your questions as well if you would like. I would love to engage in meaningful dialogue with anyone, especially those who are curious about our significance in God's plan.

I am a recovered addict. My drugs of choice were alcohol and lots of marijuana. I have been drug and alcohol free for over twenty-two years. And I hope to one day be free of my chains as well. My racial chains. My aspirational chains. My physical chains. I am forty-four years old.

I love everyone simply because I choose to. And I pray that you all will allow God to teach you to love each other. Amen.

Leslie Williams
250996, 900 Highland Ave.

Cheshire, CT. 06410

www.ingramcontent.com/pod-product-compliance
Lightning Source LLC
Chambersburg PA
CBHW071857070526
44583CB00016B/1728